Snowshoe Trails
TAHOE

THE BEST ROUTES
IN THE TAHOE SIERRA

MIKE WHITE

D1533875

WILDERNESS PRESS · BERKELEY, CA

Snowshoe Trails Tahoe: The Best Routes in the Tahoe Sierra

1st EDITION December 1998
2nd EDITION October 2005
   2nd printing September 2006

Copyright © 1998, 2005 by Mike White

Front cover photo: copyright © 2005 by Mike White
Interior photos, except where noted: Mike White
Maps: Mike White
Cover design: Larry B. Van Dyke/Lisa Pletka
Book design: Emily Douglas/Larry B. Van Dyke
Book editor: Jessica Benner

ISBN 0-89997-392-2
UPC 7-19609-97392-8

Manufactured in China

Published by: **Wilderness Press**
                1200 5th Street
                Berkeley, CA 94710
                (800) 443-7227; FAX (510) 558-1696
                info@wildernesspress.com
                www.wildernesspress.com
Visit our website for a complete listing of our books and for ordering information.

Cover photo: Snowshoer admiring the view from Lake Vista (Trip 26)
Frontispiece: Round Top from the ridge to Little Round Top (Trip 47)

DEDICATION

This guide is dedicated to my sons, David and Stephen, who are still young enough to occasionally remind their dad that snow is meant for play. May they always be child-like at heart no matter what their age.

ACKNOWLEDGMENTS

The publication of a book is seldom accomplished by a single person, as is certainly the case with this one. First and foremost, I extend my heartfelt gratitude to my wife, Robin, my faithful companion for over thirty years: for her tireless support, encouragement, and assistance, without which the publication of this guide would be totally impossible. The other principal woman in the life of this book is Caroline Winnett, the publisher at Wilderness Press, who gave birth to the original idea for the Snowshoe Trails series. Caroline's father Tom, founder of the company and my first boss at WP, provided the editing for the first edition. Jessica Benner performed exceptionally on the editing for the new edition.

Most outdoor experts advise against solitary travel in the backcountry, primarily for safety reasons. Violating this rule on many occasions, primarily out of necessity, I seem to fill any need for solitude quite easily. Therefore, the company of a good friend on the trail is a highly prized commodity. I would like to extend my thanks to all those who traveled with me through the course of this project. My good friend Chris Taylor blessed me with his presence on the majority of the trips. His steady demeanor and calm spirit were much appreciated, not to mention the breaking of several miles of trail. Dan Palmer also joined me for many excursions, the short days and cold temperatures of winter made a little brighter by his jovial nature. A number of other friends joined me on occasion, including Keith Catlin, my longtime climbing and hiking partner; Bob Redding, who further labored my already taxed respiration by his rapid-fire, unrelenting humor; Mike Wilhelm; my niece, Carmel Bang; Tim Baguley; and Jen Walters. Thanks also go to Mike Alger for his help with the weather data.

A number of Forest Service personnel answered questions and provided invaluable tidbits of information throughout the course of my research. Although they remain nameless, my thanks go to all of those who contributed their expertise.

Lastly, but most importantly, I wish to express my gratitude to the Creator for the beauty of His creation and the many blessings that allowed me the opportunity to explore the wonders of such magnificent country.

Mike White, September 2005

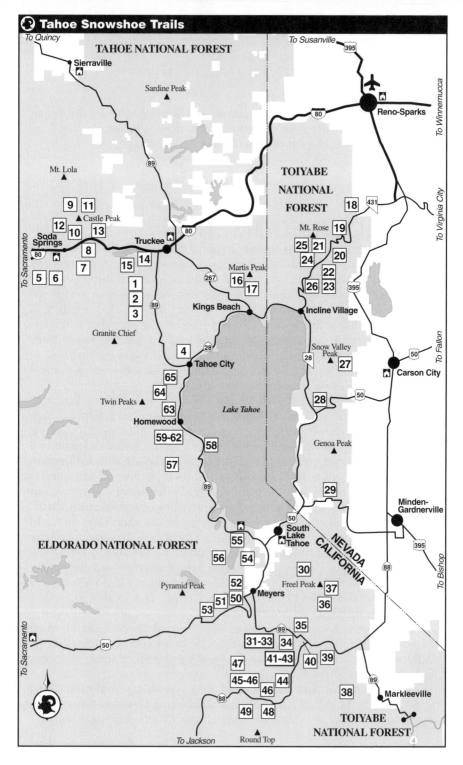

Table of Contents

I. General Information

II. Trips

Author at Page Meadows

Lake Tahoe from Peak 7572

CHAPTER 1

Introduction

Known for the crystal clarity of its deep blue waters, Lake Tahoe is the most valuable gem in the treasury of the Sierra Nevada. While jewelers measure precious stones in carats, less romantic units of measure attempt to capture the magnitude of Tahoe's greatness. Twenty-one miles long and twelve miles across, Lake Tahoe is the largest subalpine lake in North America. At a depth of 1645 feet, Tahoe is the tenth deepest lake in the world and third deepest in North America. Circling the shoreline requires a 72-mile journey. However, while numbers quantify the size of the lake, they are totally inadequate for expressing the sublime beauty of the lake and the surrounding landscape.

The large body of water was originally named Lake Bonpland by the famous western explorer, John C. Fremont, for Aimé Jacques Alexandre Bonpland, a French botanist. After first appearing on a map published in 1848, the name lasted less than a decade, replaced in 1857 by "Lake Bigler," after a former governor of California. The name "Bigler" lasted a relatively short time also, passing away as the ex-governor's reputation became sullied. By the early 1860s a groundswell began for changing the name to the current appellation. Actually, "Tahoe" is a less than perfect English adaptation of a Washoe Indian word meaning "big water." However, the meaning certainly captures the essence of the lake.

As the usually pleasant Indian summers fade into fall and in turn the autumn leaves covering the ground herald the arrival of winter, the attention of outdoor enthusiasts turns toward winter pursuits. When snow blankets the landscape, vehicle access to the mountainous terrain around Lake Tahoe becomes more limited, expanding the backcountry and opening up a whole new world of possibilities beyond the highways for those willing to travel under their own power. Deep canyons, subalpine lakes, knife-edged peaks, and incomparable views are all here in abundance, awaiting discovery by eager snowshoers. Never too far out of sight, the emerald-blue, sparkling waters of Lake Tahoe act as nature's grand mirror, reflecting the glistening snow-covered peaks circling the basin. Spectacular scenery combines with the traditionally fair Sierra weather to create a dazzling paradise for winter travelers. Snowshoers visiting the region for the first time will be awestruck by the incredible beauty around them.

Recreation is an important part of life at Lake Tahoe. Certainly, the area is Northern California's premier winter playground. Fifteen alpine ski resorts are scattered around the lake, along with a dozen cross-country ski centers and a number of snowmobile concessions. A sunny weekend will see many families from the Bay Area, the Sacramento Valley, and Reno-Sparks engaged in the winter activities of sledding down hillsides, building snowmen, or gleefully throwing snowballs at one another. Everyone loves the winters at Lake Tahoe.

Visiting Lake Tahoe in this day and age without becoming aware of the environmental concerns facing the lake is difficult. Under the banner of *"Keep Tahoe Blue,"* bumper stickers, license plates, and advertisements alert residents and visitors alike to the potential threat to the quality of life at the lake. Questions about water quality, air pollution, forest health, and overuse abound and may result in some restrictions on using the lake's resources. Presently, snowshoers visiting the Lake Tahoe Basin are free from restrictions, other than purchasing a Sno-Park permit, or a wilderness permit for entry into Desolation Wilderness. However, all outdoor users should practice minimum-impact techniques and treat the area with utmost care. Lake Tahoe and the surrounding region is a tremendous resource deserving appreciation and respect by all.

ACCESS

Lake Tahoe is surrounded by a reasonably adequate network of highways—although Bay Area residents, stuck in a crawling tangle of Sunday evening traffic on their return from a weekend of skiing, may heartily disagree with that statement. Weather permitting, the highways surrounding Lake Tahoe remain open throughout the winter. The only road vulnerable to prolonged closure is the stretch of Highway 89 on the west side of the lake around Emerald Bay. Avalanches may force the Department of Transportation (Caltrans) to close this short stretch of road at the height of winter storms. All other highways remain open, except for temporary closures during periods of intense snowfall and high winds.

Interstate 80, the east–west ribbon of federally built freeway stretching from one coast to the other, provides the principal entry from Northern California to one of America's favorite recreational playgrounds. This four-lane highway gradually climbs the west slope, crosses Donner Summit at 7227 feet above sea level, and then plunges steeply toward Reno and the Great Basin. The well-traveled Interstate is the main link between San Francisco and points east for commercial, recreational, and travel purposes. Replaced by I-80, the old two-lane highway over Donner Pass, now referred to as Donner Pass Road, was an engineering marvel at the time of construction.

The old road mostly parallels the modern Interstate, still providing unhurried motorists with exceptional scenery.

U.S. Highway 50, the first paved transcontinental road in America, is the major access at the south end of the lake. The two-lane byway brings travelers east from Sacramento, over Echo Summit at 7377 feet, and down to South Lake Tahoe. Passing through the area of the highest level of commercialism on the lake, a four-lane stretch of Highway 50 skirts the south and southeast shores before climbing briefly over Spooner Summit and then descending precipitously to Carson City. Of the three major east–west highways providing access to the lake, U.S. 50 is the only one of the trio that actually reaches the shores of Tahoe.

Leaving the Sacramento Valley, California State Route 88 leads through the small community of Jackson and follows a winding path on the way to Carson Pass, just over 15 air miles from the south shore of Lake Tahoe. At 8593 feet, Carson Pass is the highest summit of the three major east–west highways providing access to the lake. The relatively high elevation, coupled with the favorable topography near the pass, creates a winter wonderland for recreationists. Continuing beyond the apex of the route, the two-lane highway drops dramatically east to Carson Valley and the Nevada towns of Minden and Gardnerville.

A continuous band of pavement creates a rough oval around the entire shoreline of Lake Tahoe. Although composed of segments of four separate highways (CA 89, U.S. 50, NV 28, & CA 28), in essence the route is an uninterrupted loop road all the way around the lake. Various secondary highways, along with previously mentioned Highway 50, make connections from beyond Tahoe to this lakeshore loop. From the quaint town of Truckee, two roads leave Interstate 80 and connect to this loop at its north end. From the west end of Truckee, Highway 89 follows the course of the Truckee River, past turnoffs to Squaw Valley and Alpine Meadows, and on to the river's emergence from the lake at the gates in Tahoe City. Heading southeast from Truckee, Highway 267 climbs over Brockway Summit and then descends to Kings Beach.

From the south end of Reno, Nevada Highway 431 leaves U.S. 395 and climbs steeply past the Mt. Rose Ski Area and over Mt. Rose Summit, at 8933 feet the highest winter-maintained highway to cross the Sierra. From the pass, the highway drops quickly to Nevada Highway 28 near the lakeside community of Incline Village. To the south of NV 431, U.S. 50 links Carson City to South Lake Tahoe before leaving the basin at Echo Summit as previously described. Known locally as Kingsbury Grade, Nevada State Route 207 climbs steeply from Carson Valley over Daggett Pass to a connection with U.S. 50 at Stateline. Finally, at the south end of the lake, California Highway 89 connects the Carson Pass Highway (CA 88) to South Lake Tahoe by climbing over 7735-foot Luther Pass.

TRANSPORTATION

AUTOMOBILES

As in most recreation areas of the West, access to the snowshoe trails described in this book is primarily by private automobile. Recent high-level federal discussions, centered on environmental issues related to improving the health of Lake Tahoe, hinted at the possibility of restricting private vehicle access to areas within the Lake Tahoe Basin. Currently, no limitations exist and you are free to drive on approved roads anywhere around the lake. However, no one knows what limitations the future might bring.

MASS TRANSIT

Aside from driving to trailheads in your car, few alternatives currently exist for those who are without a vehicle or would prefer to utilize public transportation, despite the advanced nature of civilization around the lake. TART (Tahoe Area Regional Transportation) offers bus service from Tahoe City to the west and north shores of the lake and to the town of Truckee. Buses are equipped with ski racks during the winter months. Call (530) 550-1212 or (800) 736-6365 for schedules and additional information. Information can also be obtained on the web at www.placer.ca.gov/works/tart/tart.htm. The following trailheads described in this book can be accessed by TART:

TRIP	BUS STOP	BUS ROUTE
1. Pole Creek & Bradley Hut	Campgrounds/Highway 89	Tahoe City/Truckee
2. Silver Peak	Campgrounds/Highway 89	Tahoe City/Truckee
3. Alpine Mdws/5 Lakes	River Ranch*	Tahoe City/Truckee
4. Tahoe City to Truckee Canyon Viewpoint	Tahoe City Y	Tahoe City/Truckee
58. Sugar Pine Point SP	Sugar Pine Point State Park	Tahoma to Incline Village
59. General Creek	Sugar Pine Point State Park	Tahoma to Incline Village
60. McKinney Lakes	Sugar Pine Point State Park	Tahoma to Incline Village
61. Richardson Lake	Sugar Pine Point State Park	Tahoma to Incline Village
62. Buck Lake	Sugar Pine Point State Park	Tahoma to Incline Village
63. Blackwood Canyon	Skyland Beach	Tahoma to Incline Village
64. Stanford Rock	Skyland Beach	Tahoma to Incline Village

*A ski shuttle provides a connection with the TART bus stop at River Ranch on Hwy. 89 to Alpine Meadows resort.

SKI SHUTTLE BUSES

A variety of shuttle buses extend services to most of Tahoe's downhill and cross-country ski resorts from both the Reno/Tahoe International Airport and major Lake Tahoe casinos and hotels. The only trips in this guide close to shuttle destinations are Trip 49 (Emigrant Lake), which begins directly across Highway 88 from the Kirkwood Cross-Country Center, and Trip 3 (Alpine Meadows to Five Lakes) as shown in the chart above. The bus to Kirkwood leaves from various properties in South Shore and cost $5.00 per person in 2005. Call (800) 446-6128 for information.

CASINO SHUTTLE BUSES

Frontier operates 14 daily shuttles between casinos in Reno and those near South Lake Tahoe. In 2005 the fare was $20 one-way and $36 round trip (local residents pay $26 round trip). Call (800) 446-6128 for information.

BUS LINES

Greyhound offers service to Truckee and Reno. Call (800) 229-9494 or visit the website at **www.greyhound.com** for more information

RAILROADS

Amtrak's California Zephyr makes daily stops in Truckee and Colfax, westbound from Reno-Sparks and eastbound from the major California centers of the Bay Area and Sacramento ((800) USA-RAIL or **www.amtrak.com**).

AIRPORTS

The Reno-Tahoe International Airport (**www.renoairport.com**), located within Reno off U.S. 395, is the major commercial airport serving the Lake Tahoe area. Commercial airlines flying into Reno-Tahoe include:

ALASKA: (800) 426-0333, www.alaska-air.com

ALOHA: (800) 367-5250, www.alohaairlines.com

AMERICA WEST: (800) 235-9292, www.americawest.com

AMERICAN: (800) 433-7300, www.aa.com

CONTINENTAL: (800) 525-0280, www.flycontinental.com

DELTA: (800) 433-9417, www.connectionbyskywest.com

NORTHWEST: (800) 225-2525, www.nwa.com

SOUTHWEST: (800) 435-9792, www.southwest.com

UNITED/UNITED EXPRESS: (800) 241-6522, www.ual.com

MUNICIPAL AIRPORTS

Carson City, Douglas County (Gardnerville), Truckee-Tahoe, and Lake Tahoe (South Lake Tahoe) airports are all light-duty facilities, primarily for private aircraft. The Lake Tahoe airport provides limited commercial shuttle services.

RENTAL CARS

A variety of companies offer cars for rent from Reno-Tahoe International Airport, South Shore, Truckee, and Incline Village.

INCLINE VILLAGE

ALPINE AUTO RENTAL: (775) 833-4424

RENO-TAHOE INTERNATIONAL AIRPORT

ALAMO: (800) 327-9633, www.goalamo.com

AVIS: (800) 984-8840, www.avis.com

BUDGET: (800) 527-0700, www.budget.com

DOLLAR: (800) 800-4000, www.dollar.com

ENTERPRISE: (800) 736-8222, www.enterprise.com

HERTZ: (800) 654-3131, www.hertz.com

NATIONAL: (800) 227-7368, www.nationalcar.com

THRIFTY: (800) 367-2277, www.thrifty.com

SOUTH SHORE

AVIS: (800) 984-8840, www.avis.com

DOLLAR: (800) 800-4000, www.dollar.com

ENTERPRISE: (800) 736-8222, www.enterprise.com

HERTZ: (800) 654-3131, www.hertz.com

NATIONAL: (800) 227-7368, www.nationalcar.com

TAHOE VALLEY AUTO: (530) 541-7830

TRUCKEE

AIRPORT AUTO RENTAL: (800) 200-2688

LAKESIDE TOWING & AUTO RENTAL: (530) 587-6000

NATIONAL: (530) 587-6748, www.nationalcar.com

THRIFTY: (800) 367-2277, www.thrifty.com

TRUCKEE RENT-A-CAR: (530) 587-2841

LODGING

A plethora of lodging options are available in and around Lake Tahoe, particularly if money is no object. A thorough discussion of the vast array of accommodations could fill a whole book, running the gamut from rustic mountain lodges to extravagant casino hotels. If you are clueless as to where to lay your head at night around the Tahoe Basin, throw yourself on the mercy of your local travel agent.

CAMPGROUNDS

The winter snows close most of the government and private campgrounds that service thousands of summer visitors. However, a few do remain open year-round.

SUGAR PINE POINT STATE PARK: On the west shore, 2.5 miles south of Homewood. Fee = $20. (530) 525-7232, www.parks.ca.gov.

ZEPHYR COVE: On the east shore, 4 miles north of Stateline. Fee = $16–24. (775) 589-4907, www.tahoedixie2.com.

LAKESIDE MOBILE HOME & RV PARK: In South Lake Tahoe, 3 miles west of Stateline on Cedar Ave. Fee = $29. (530) 544-4704.

GROVER HOT SPRINGS STATE PARK: About 3 miles west of Markleeville. Fee = $20. (530) 694-2249, www.parks.ca.gov.

DAVIS CREEK COUNTY PARK: On S.R. 429 west of U.S. 395, approximately 15 miles south of Reno. Fee = $15. (775) 849-0684, www.washoecountyparks.com.

WASHOE LAKE STATE PARK: On S.R. 428 west of U.S. 395, approximately 7 miles north of Carson City. Fee = $15. (775) 687-4319, www.parks.nv.gov.

RESTAURANTS

Tahoe offers a wide range of dining experiences in similarly overwhelming quantities to the choices for lodgings. The spectrum runs from the ubiquitous fast-food chains to the upper limits of fine dining. The "Warm-ups" heading accompanying each trail description offers suggestions for a unique culinary experience at a reasonable cost.

On ridge to Becker Peak

CHAPTER 2

Winter Travel

Having lived at the east base of the Sierra since 1976, a half hour away by car from the north shore of Lake Tahoe, I have seen a number of winters. The one conclusion I have reached regarding the weather is that "normal" is a statistical average that rarely coincides with the real world. During the past thirty years, the weather has run the climatic spectrum, from El Niños to multi-year droughts, with everything in between. During drought periods, walking the trails on bare ground was possible in some winter months, while in other years even reaching the lake was impossible for days due to overwhelming snowfall.

WEATHER

Despite the scientific advances in weather forecasting, from year to year you just do not know what the winter will be like until the season progresses. However, reliable, short-term weather forecasts are easily available to virtually anyone with a computer, phone, or television. A list of appropriate weather forecast sources for the Lake Tahoe region is in Appendix I. The wise recreationist uses available weather information in planning any trip.

Wild variations aside, the climate of Lake Tahoe can be classified on the whole as dry. The sun shines 84% of the time, an average of 307 days per year. Many an ideal trip occurs during days of bright sunshine following a storm that blanketed the Sierra with a layer of fresh powder.

Most winter storms bringing moisture to the Tahoe Sierra plow into the range from the west, dropping snow on the higher elevations before moving east across the Great Basin. Most storms last no more than a day or two, separated by periods of dry, sunny weather. However, severe storms lasting for days and dropping incredible amounts of snow are not uncommon, particularly as the winters of '97–'98 and '04–'05 have shown. Some days the weather at Lake Tahoe is idyllic, some days life-threatening. Remember, nearby is where the epic struggle of the Donner Party took place.

Average yearly snowfall is nearly 190 inches at lake level, substantially greater at the higher elevations (ski resorts report 300–500 inches per year).

Typically, snow falls between November and April, although the heaviest snow comes from December through March. Snowfall has been recorded in every month at Lake Tahoe. Winter temperatures are relatively mild, the average high around 40 degrees and the average low near 20 degrees.

AVERAGE TEMPERATURE & SNOWFALL CHART

	NOV	DEC	JAN	FEB	MAR	APR
AVG. HIGH TEMP.	46.9°	40.8°	34.9°	41.5°	43.9°	50.4°
AVG. LOW TEMP.	26.2°	20.8°	19.6°	20.7°	23.2°	27.0°
AVG. SNOW DEPTH	3"	11"	21"	31"	28"	14"
AVG. SNOWFALL	16.4"	34.3"	43.8"	37.6"	36.0"	15.0"

Measurements recorded for Tahoe City, California

Although firm guarantees are non-existent, sunshine and mild temperatures are a reasonable expectation for a day of snowshoeing in the Tahoe Sierra. However, you must be prepared for any condition—sunshine, snow, sleet, rain, wind, and cold all can be extreme at one time or another. Wild variations may even occur during the same day. Residents commenting on the climate to outsiders will often be heard to say, "If you don't like the weather, wait five minutes." Make sure you have the appropriate clothing and equipment to successfully endure whatever conditions you might possibly encounter.

SEASON

The winter snowpack varies greatly from year to year, making accurate predictions of the optimum time for snowshoeing difficult. Typically, there is enough snow at lake level and above for decent snowshoeing from December through March. During years of abundant snowfall, the season can be extended to include an early start in November and a late finish in April. Since Lake Tahoe hosts a plethora of ski resorts, obtaining accurate information on current conditions is fairly easy.

Snow conditions around the lake will vary, due to a number of different factors. Obviously, altitude is an important determiner of the quantity and quality of the snowpack. During warm weather, the snow around the shores of Lake Tahoe, at an elevation of 6200 feet, may be a wet mush or gone altogether, while at Carson Pass, over 2000 feet higher, conditions might be ideal. Geographical location also plays a significant part in snowfall distribution. As Pacific storms approach the Sierra from the ocean, more snow is deposited on the west side of the range than along the east slope. Conditions are also determined by exposure. South-facing slopes are the first to lose their snow, followed by west-, east-, and finally north-facing slopes. Forested areas, protected from the direct rays of the sun, will hang onto their snow longer than open meadows and exposed hillsides. Topography, wind, and micro-climates are additional factors influencing the nature of the snowpack, making a firm prediction for the season of use a highly variable speculation.

When determining the best time for a particular trip, you must consider all these factors. Consult the weather, avalanche, and ski reports for current conditions before your trip. Most Forest Service ranger stations have useful information.

ROUTEFINDING

No backcountry skill is more important in winter than the ability to find your way over snow-covered terrain. There are no trails to follow, at least none built into the soil and maintained by the government, as you will find in the summer. Unless you have the luxury of following a marked trail or the tracks of a previous party, you must be able to interpret major and minor features of the terrain, read a map, and navigate through the backcountry for most of the trips in this book. Space does not allow for a dissertation on the necessary elements of navigation, orientation, and routefinding, so you must gather a good understanding of this subject from other sources. The following principles should serve as an outline of a more detailed comprehension of this art.

- Always study your route carefully before you leave home
- Always leave a detailed description of your proposed route with a reliable person
- Always carry a topographic map of the area
- Always carry a compass and/or GPS receiver
- Constantly observe the terrain as you progress
- If necessary, mark your trail (and remove your markers on the return)
- Always keep your party together as you travel

A GPS receiver is helpful for determining your position in the backcountry. However, no piece of equipment is an adequate replacement for the skills of navigation, orientation, and routefinding.

OBJECTIVE HAZARDS

SUN

For most people, the best days to be snowshoeing in the mountains are when the snow is fresh and the skies are blue. Unfortunately, these conditions produce their own set of problems: sun, snow, and altitude combine to create the perfect reflective oven for baking exposed skin. However, winter usually finds snowshoers fully covered by some sort of apparel, with the exception of the face. Remember to apply an effective sunblock to all exposed areas of your skin before venturing out onto snow-covered terrain in the intense winter sun. Reapply the sunblock as necessary throughout the duration of the trip.

Snow blindness is a very real problem at these elevations in the winter. This malady is caused by prolonged exposure of the eyes to ultraviolet rays. Always wear a pair of goggles or sunglasses that filter out at least 90% of UVA and UVB rays, particularly on clear and sunny days. In addition, side shields on glasses will help to reduce reflective rays.

DEHYDRATION

Becoming dehydrated in the midst of so much frozen liquid may seem ludicrous, but without enough water to replenish reserves, a vigorous activity like snowshoeing can put you in danger of just such a problem. Lots of moisture can be lost during strenuous exercise in cold, dry weather simply through respiration. Always carry plenty of water—most streams and lakes are frozen, and eating snow is an inadequate long-term solution.

If open water happens to be found, bear in mind that many water sources in the Tahoe area may be contaminated with pathogens. All water should be treated, even the clearest-looking.

ALTITUDE

Most elevations around the Tahoe area are not extreme. However, some people, particularly those who live near sea level, may suffer the effects of altitude sickness and its more serious counterpart, acute mountain sickness. Symptoms of altitude sickness include headache, fatigue, loss of appetite, shortness of breath, nausea, vomiting, drowsiness, dizziness, memory loss, and loss of mental acuity. Although rare at these elevations, acute mountain sickness is possible. It requires immediate descent and medical attention.

To avoid these maladies, drink plenty of fluids, eat a diet high in carbohydrates prior to and during a trip, and acclimatize slowly. A rapid descent will usually resolve any of the aforementioned symptoms. A severe case of altitude sickness is unlikely at these elevations during one-day trips, although not impossible.

COLD

Hypothermia is a condition in which the human body's core temperature drops below normal in response to prolonged exposure to cold. Air temperature is not always the determining factor, as many cases of hypothermia occur when the thermometer registers above freezing. Wind chill, fatigue, and wetness (from rain, melting snow, submersion, or even excessive perspiration) can contribute to hypothermia.

The best solution for avoiding hypothermia is prevention. Do not get too cold, too tired, or too wet. Dress in layers and take time to adjust your clothing as conditions change, preventing yourself from becoming too cold as well as impeding excessive wetness, from either precipitation or perspiration. Refrain from pushing on toward exhaustion when tired. Drink plenty of fluids and eat enough energy-producing food. Carry extra clothes in your vehicle to change into after a trip. If you suspect one of your party is experiencing the symptoms of hypothermia, handle the situation immediately. Due to the loss of mental acuity, you will not be able to detect symptoms in yourself.

Frostbite, a condition where tissue actually freezes after prolonged exposure to the cold, is a potential concern during cold weather. Most susceptible to frostbite are the feet, hands, face, and ears. Adequate equipment, including properly fitting footwear, warm socks, gloves, and hat should counteract the prolonged cold that can cause this malady.

AVALANCHES

Certainly, the most impressive winter hazard in the backcountry is the avalanche. Space does not allow for a complete discussion of avalanches here, and you should read as much as you can about them (see Suggested Reading in Appendix IV: *Mountaineering: The Freedom of the Hills*, *ABC of Avalanche Safety*, *Allen & Mike's Really Cool Backcountry Ski Book*, and *Snowshoeing*). Avalanches usually occur due to instability between the surface layer and the underlying snow, which can exist for a variety of reasons. They most commonly occur during and soon after storms, and during periods of rising temperatures, but are not limited to these times.

The most avalanche-prone areas include gullies, slopes between 30 and 45 degrees, north-facing slopes in winter, south-facing slopes in spring, lee slopes, treeless slopes, and slopes where younger trees are bordered by more mature forest. In addition, hillsides with a convex slope are prone to fracture more easily than ones with a concave slope. As much as possible, avoid these areas, particularly during periods of instability.

Even small avalanches pack a considerable wallop. Many years ago after a successful spring climb in the Sawtooth Ridge above Twin Lakes, we decided to glissade down a snow-filled gully for our return route. After a prolonged period of questioning the wisdom of the descent, I dropped to my butt and pushed off down the gully. About halfway down the slope I felt some pressure on my back and instantly started to somersault down the gully. I came to rest at the base of the slope, stripped of my hat, gloves and pack, which were now scattered haphazardly across the snow. My outer parka was halfway over my head and snow filled every available passageway through my remaining clothing. Once I gathered my wits and surveyed the situation, I realized that this tremendous force, which tossed me and my

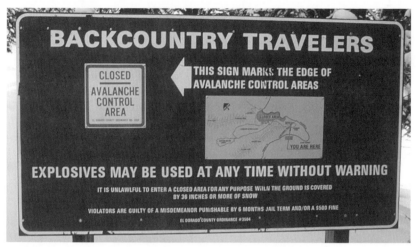

Avalanche warning sign

equipment all over the mountain, was created by an avalanche a mere 12 inches high and 6 feet across.

Many people have put forth theories about what to do if caught in an avalanche. My own experience, along with reports from others caught in similar circumstances, has led me to believe that most avalanches occur far too quickly and with too much force for a victim to do much of anything. However, conventional wisdom dictates that you should try to get on your back with your head uphill and make a swimming motion with your arms in an attempt to stay on top of the avalanche or work your way toward the edge. Good luck. Like so many things in this life, the best cure is to avoid the disease.

Although there is no substitute for a wide range of winter experience in determining avalanche risk, there are some guidelines which you would be wise to follow when traveling in the backcountry.

MINIMIZING AVALANCHE DANGER

1. Obtain the current avalanche report for this area (530) 587-2158.
2. Select the safest route—follow ridges wherever possible.
3. Test slopes for stability. (See Appendix IV for resources on appropriate procedures).
4. Travel through suspect terrain quickly, one at a time, from safety zone to safety zone.
5. Carry the proper equipment & know how to use it. (Necessary equipment may include shovels, probes, beacons, avalanche cord, cellular phone, first-aid kit).

CORNICES

Another impressive feature of the winter landscape is the cornice, an over-hanging mass of snow at the crest of a ridge formed where prevailing winds drift snowfall leeward over the edge. Cornices pose two problems. Eventually and without warning, cornices will break off and plunge to the slope below, and falling cornices can trigger avalanches on unstable slopes. Obviously, the larger the cornice, the greater the potential for damage. A less obvious danger arises when you travel along a ridge: If you snowshoe on the corniced edge of a ridge, you may go for a sudden and perhaps final ride.

Cornice on Little Round Top

TRAIL ETIQUETTE

In general, trail etiquette is much the same in winter as in summer.

1. AVOID SNOWSHOEING ON EXISTING CROSS-COUNTRY SKI TRACKS—this allows skiers to reuse their tracks for return trips and provides an existing track for future users.

2. YIELD THE RIGHT OF WAY TO SNOWMOBILES & CROSS-COUNTRY SKIERS—granting the lane to snowmobiles is purely common sense. A person on snowshoes will never win a standoff with a snowmobile. As for skiers, a snowshoer usually has more control over his or her movements than people on skis.

3. PACK OUT ALL LITTER—Winter, summer, spring, or fall, all garbage should be removed from the backcountry.

No Snowmobile sign

4. KEEP PETS AND THEIR PRODUCTS UNDER CONTROL—If you choose to share the backcountry with your dog, make sure it is a reasonably sociable animal. Chances are you will meet other dogs and other people on the trail, and nothing is more undesirable than having to break up a fight between animals or personally fend off unfriendly canines. Please scatter their droppings as well. Popular trails can become quite unkempt between snowfalls.

SANITATION

Winter presents a whole new situation for dealing with the proper disposal of waste materials. Urinating is fairly straightforward—as long as you don't pee into the snow above a frozen lake or stream. Visual appearance is the main consideration. Whereas urine will soak into the summer soil without a trace, snow will take on varying shades of yellow depending on the concentration of the urine. Find a spot well off the trail or a good distance away from a campsite to avoid the resulting visual pollution.

Defecating in the winter backcountry is not nearly as benign as urinating. Short of removing the waste altogether, which remains to most of us an undesirable alternative, there is no adequate way to dispose of waste products that doesn't adversely affect the environment. Burying stool in warmer times of the year allows the waste to gradually decompose and, when a suitable site is chosen, provides minimal risk of groundwater contamination. The danger in winter is that you will select a site where spring thaws cause an excessive amount of poop to find its way into the groundwater or a stream. Some experts speculate that the spread of giardia in the backcountry is due primarily to poor sanitation practices of winter users.

So what should we do? Taking care of your business at home before or after a trip avoids the problem altogether. However, if nature calls at a less convenient time, the best solution is to pack it out. For those who are not blessed with the ability to regulate their stools and have no desire to pack around their own poop, there are a few guidelines to practice. First of all, visual pollution is certainly a concern with site selection—pick a site well away from potential discovery by others. Nothing ruins the winter landscape more quickly than the unfortunate discovery of a previous traveler's waste products staining the snow. Second, as best you can, choose a location that obviously won't contaminate a water source. Third, find a southern exposure and try to place your results just below the surface. This allows the freeze-thaw cycle the opportunity to begin breaking down the stool as best as possible, as well as helping to dilute the waste products over the course of the spring melt.

What about used toilet paper? Once again, the best solution is to pack it out. Burning your toilet paper as recommended for backcountry users in other seasons becomes fairly impractical during the winter. Carrying out your used paper seems somewhat less obnoxious than packing out the stool. Remember, the minor inconvenience is outweighed by the greater good.

Although this guide is primarily concerned with day trips, overnight users should use consideration when disposing of waste water and any leftover food.

PERMITS

WILDERNESS PERMITS

Desolation Wilderness: Permits are required for day use as well as overnight stays. Day-users may pick up free permits at either the Lake Tahoe Basin Management Unit or the Eldorado Information Center during office hours (M–F, 8 A.M.–4:30 P.M.), or self-register after hours. For overnight stays, you must pick up and pay for your permit in person during office hours. The fee is $5.00 per person per night for the first 2 nights. The Forest Service may elect to mail overnight permits on a per case basis but doing so is not now established policy. Campfires are not allowed in the wilderness at any time.

Trips in this book entering Desolation Wilderness include Ralston Peak (Trip 53) and Mt. Tallac (Trip 56). For more information, contact:

Lake Tahoe Visitor Center
Lake Tahoe Basin Management Unit
870 Emerald Bay Road
South Lake Tahoe, CA 96150
(530) 573-2674
www.fs.fed.us/r5/ltbmu/

Pacific Ranger District
Eldorado National Forest
7887 Highway 50
Pollack Pines, CA 95726
(530) 644-6048
www.fs.fed.us/r5/Eldorado/

Mokelumne Wilderness: Permits are not required at this time for winter use.

CALIFORNIA SNO-PARK PERMITS

For many years the State of California has utilized the Sno-Park program to provide vehicle parking and access to popular winter recreational areas. Day permits cost $5.00 and a season pass is $25.00. They can be obtained from a variety of commercial establishments and visitor information centers. Along with parking space, Sno-Parks include sanitation facilities, but do not allow overnight camping. Vehicles parked in a Sno-Park without a permit properly displayed on the dashboard are subject to a $75.00 fine. Call (916) 324-1222 or visit **www.ohv.parks.ca.gov** for more information. The following Sno-Parks serve as trailheads for snowshoe trips in this book:

SNO-PARK	TRIPS	INFORMATION
DONNER SUMMIT	8–13	USFS (530) 587-3558
DONNER MEMORIAL STATE PARK	14–15	DMSP (530) 582-7892
MEISS MEADOW	44–47	USFS (209) 295-4251
CARSON PASS	48	USFS (209) 295-4251
ECHO LAKE	50–52	USFS (530) 573-2600
TAYLOR CREEK	55	USFS (530) 573-2600
BLACKWOOD CANYON	63–64	USFS (530) 573-2600

Additional Sno-Parks in the Lake Tahoe region are located at Yuba Gap, Yuba Pass, Cisco Grove, and Echo Summit.

CHAPTER 3

Equipment

The early Seventies saw a significant change in the design and composition of snowshoes. Before this era, the typical snowshoe was constructed from raw materials of wood and leather. With names like "bearpaw" and "beavertail" describing the classic shapes, outdoorsmen plodded through the snow with altered strides and rangy motions. Most of these predecessors of the modern snowshoe were large and cumbersome. They provided adequate flotation by utilizing a large surface area, which forced users to compensate for their wide and long dimensions by adopting a gait reminiscent of a cowboy walking away from his horse after a long day's ride. In this present era, these old classics are more likely found nailed to the rough-wood paneled walls of a mountain cabin or café, than on the backcountry snow. Traditionalists may find a diminishing selection of suppliers who still provide the old wooden snowshoe for sale.

SNOWSHOES

Taking advantage of modern materials, new designs have revolutionized the manufacture of snowshoes (find a list of suppliers in the Appendix III). Lightweight metals, space-age-plastics, and other substances have enabled designers to create lighter, smaller and more efficient snowshoes that are far easier to use. Rather than the cumbersome, oversized snowshoes of old, trim shoes with modern traction devices allow recreationists to pursue their sport with ease over a greater variety of terrain. High-angled slopes that would have been next to impossible for traditional shoes are commonly ascended and descended successfully with the newer equipment. The advanced design of snowshoes has definitely made the winter landscape more accessible by users of all skill levels.

Most modern snowshoes fall into the category known as western, named for their origin in the mountain west. Designed for efficient travel over mountainous terrain, western snowshoes are generally smaller and lighter than their traditional counterparts. Although some molded models have had recent success, most western snowshoes have a tubular metal frame and some type of synthetic decking. Advanced bindings are attached to the snowshoe at a single flex point, and have traction devices that are well-suited for icy or hard-packed snow conditions.

Manufacturers provide different snowshoes for different types of snow, but most snowshoers will try to get by with a single pair. With prices averaging well over $200 per pair, purchasing different sets for a variety of snow conditions may be a luxury. One manufacturer has overcome the cost barrier to owning more than a single pair by making interchangeable tails that can be added or taken off the main shoe to adapt the length to different snow conditions. When buying a set of shoes, make a choice that will meet your needs for most of the conditions you are likely to see in the backcountry.

Snowshoeing in the Sierra can present recreationists with a wide variety of snow types. Soft, fluffy powder is most often encountered after a storm, with snowfalls of up to 4 feet not uncommon. During these periods, enthusiasts are likely to crave the largest snowshoe they can strap to their feet. Once the snow becomes consolidated, users turn their attention to smaller shoes with greater maneuverability. During hard-pack conditions users want the smallest shoe available with the best traction devices. The spring season presents possibly the greatest challenge, when snow is firm early in the day but turns to wet mush in the afternoon sun.

Selecting the best snowshoe to cover all the possibilities can be daunting. In general, try to get by with the smallest shoe that will reasonably han-

Snowshoe equipment

dle the many types of snow you will encounter in the backcountry. If planning to backpack with snowshoes, you will need a larger size than ones used simply for day trips. For those users who want to climb over steep terrain, a lightweight, smaller shoe with a good traction device is the best choice. If money is no object, buy as many shoes as you will need for the variety of situations you will encounter. For the rest of you, make a careful assessment of your needs and make a decision to buy one or two pairs of snowshoes that will handle most of the situations you expect to find.

POLES

Ski poles are an important item that some people elect not to use, but for most snowshoers they provide an extra measure of stability in keeping oneself upright. In addition, they provide the upper body with a certain degree of exercise and bear some portion of the load that your legs would otherwise carry alone. Some poles can be threaded together when their baskets are removed, thereby doubling as avalanche probes.

CLOTHING

The backcountry rule of thumb for clothing is summed up in one word—layering. Many layers of lightweight clothing allow greater flexibility to adapt to the changing conditions of strenuous exercise in winter. Adding or subtracting layers helps the backcountry user regulate his or her body temperature more easily than a few thick layers of clothing.

BOOTS

Protecting your feet from the cold temperatures and potentially wet conditions of winter is of the utmost importance. Many snowshoe trips, starting out as pleasant excursions into winter wonderlands, have turned into living nightmares due to agonizingly wet and bitterly cold feet. Not too long ago there weren't many options for footwear in the snowshoeing world. Whatever hiking boots you used during the summer were the same ones you would strap into your snowshoes in the winter, properly coated with multiple applications of some waxy sealant in a less than totally effective attempt to keep your feet dry. Nowadays, a number of companies are producing winter-type boots suitable for many outdoor pursuits, some more appropriate for snowshoeing than others.

Winterizing one's summer boots is still an option that many continue to pursue and one that is quite effective in the spring part of the season. If you choose to do this, make sure that your footwear is substantial enough to provide adequate support and comfort when attached to a pair of snowshoes. Fortunately, the Lake Tahoe area does not see the number of bitterly cold days that some regions of the country suffer, but still your boots must provide a moderate level of warmth. In addition you must protect your boots sufficiently from wetness, particularly in the spring, when warm days begin to turn the snowpack into a wet mush. Consult your local backcountry retailer for the best water-protection product for your particular type of boot.

If you decide to use winter boots, select a pair that will provide the necessary rigidity required for successful operation of your snowshoes. Many winter boots are designed for walking around in the snow, but are not necessarily made for snowshoeing. Some models come with felt-type liners for extra protection from the cold—make sure if you purchase a pair that these boots fit appropriately with and without the liners. Talk to an informed clerk at a reliable outdoor store for their recommendations.

GAITERS
A good pair of gaiters is a winter essential for keeping snow out of your boots. Select gaiters that are made from durable fabrics and are easy to put on and remove.

SOCKS
Socks are probably the most important piece of clothing when it comes to keeping you warm. There seems to be as many sock combinations as there are backcountry users, so pick a mixture that works best for you. Select liners from synthetic fabrics that will pass moisture easily to the outer sock layers. Outer socks should be thicker wool or synthetic blends which can keep your feet warm even when wet.

UNDERWEAR
Many synthetic materials have been developed for use in the backcountry. Select types that will conduct perspiration to your outer layers of clothing quickly while maintaining an ability to keep you warm. As nice as cotton feels against your skin, once it gets wet, you get cold.

PANTS
Choose pants made from synthetic materials or wool that are lightweight, loose-fitting, water-resistant and durable. A pair of nylon shell pants over your regular pants will help to shed snow and protect your legs from the wind. Gore-Tex or an equivalent material will help keep you dry in wet conditions.

TORSO
Modern fabrics have greatly aided the outdoor world in keeping recreationists warm and dry. Once again, multiple layers allow you to adjust to changing conditions whether they be external or internal fluctuations in temperature. With the advent of pile, fleece, and other synthetic products, the snowshoer has a wide range of choices for what to wear around the upper body next to the primary layer of underwear. Shirts, vests, pullovers,

and jackets can all be used alone or interchangeably to achieve comfort. Down-filled vests and jackets are still popular choices for warmth, lightweight, and compressibility—just make sure they don't get wet. Your outer layer should be a waterproof or water-resistant parka with a hood that will protect you from wind and weather.

HATS
In the Sierra you will most likely need two hats. The first should protect you from the intense rays of the sun on those idyllic, clear days. Baseball-style hats are well-suited to filling this need, as long as you provide additional protection for the neck and ears. When it's cold you will need to keep your head warm. A stocking hat that can adjust to provide protection for your face also during extreme conditions is an excellent choice.

GLOVES/MITTS
Next to cold feet, cold hands can make you nearly as miserable in the backcountry. Mitts will keep your hands warmer than gloves. Usually the best combination for handwear consists of an inner liner of synthetic material or wool and an outer shell made of waterproof nylon reinforced in critical areas with a more durable fabric.

SAFETY DEVICES

AVALANCHE BEACONS
If you expect to travel extensively through potential avalanche terrain, a set of avalanche beacons is a wise choice. To be effective, everyone in your party must carry a device and be trained in its use. Batteries should always be checked prior to your departure and an extra set carried in your pack.

AVALANCHE CORD
A less expensive alternative to beacons, avalanche cord is a thin, hundred-foot-long cord that snowshoers secure to their bodies at equal intervals. In the event of an avalanche, rescuers can follow an exposed section of cord to the victim.

AVALANCHE PROBES
Probes aid in finding a buried victim. The most efficient way to carry avalanche probes is to have ski poles that will connect into a single probe. Teammates can pierce the snowpack with the probes in search of victims.

SNOW SHOVELS
Everyone in your party should carry a lightweight snow shovel. Not only essential in avalanche rescue, snow shovels are of immense help if you have to construct a temporary shelter.

CELLULAR PHONES

Technology has produced many wonderful gadgets designed to make our lives easier, although I am not sure that statement always applies to cellular phones. Personal pet peeves aside, cellular phones do provide an instant link with the outside world in case of an emergency, provided you're in an area of service. As long they are not abused, cellular phones can be a tremendous resource in times of real trouble.

NAVIGATIONAL AIDS

Obviously, snow-cover is the most significant distinction of the Tahoe Sierra in winter when compared to the summer landscape. While hikers and backpackers, without much thought, typically follow a well-defined trail to their favorite destination during the summer months, winter travelers are governed by a much different set of circumstances. In the absence of the established trails of summer, a modicum of navigational skill is necessary to safely negotiate the snow-covered backcountry. Trail signs and blazes on trees are lost, and even dominant physical characteristics, such as streams and lakes, can disappear or be significantly altered by a normal snowpack. In order to successfully negotiate the winter landscape, you must have certain equipment and a sufficient knowledge of its use.

GPS SYSTEMS

With the advent of access to the GPS system by the general public, many outdoor lovers have come to depend upon hand-held monitors for accurately locating their position in the backcountry. Particularly in the winter, when trails and landmarks become obscured by the deepening snows of winter, GPS devices can be a great asset, although certainly not an absolute necessity. In densely forested terrain or during inclement weather, the ability to use this technology can save you from aimlessly wandering through the mountains, which could lead to much more severe consequences. However, a GPS device is no substitute for backcountry savvy and the knowledge of how to read the landscape coupled with the ability to read a map and use a compass.

MAP & COMPASS

When traveling through mountain snows, a USGS 7.5-minute topographic map is an essential element for your pack, especially when journeying along unmarked routes. Typically, these maps provide the user with detailed topographic information, including contours, elevations of important landmarks, and the location of physical characteristics such as streams, lakes, mountains, and canyons. As with many tools, these maps are next to useless without an understanding of them. If you lack the necessary skill or experience to use these maps, you may be able to gain it through programs of local outdoor groups, through adult education courses, or by consulting an appropriate publication.

In addition to these USGS maps, a number of other maps cover the Lake Tahoe region. The Forest Service publishes topographic maps on plastic film for both Desolation Wilderness and Mokelumne Wilderness that are at an adequate scale for backcountry navigation. The Forest Service provides additional maps of its districts, but they lack topographic information and are at too small a scale to be used for backcountry travel. Similarly, numerous recreation maps are published by private companies, but they also lack the necessary scale for finding your way in the wild. There is no good substitute for the USGS maps.

A map covering the area of your travel is a necessary item, but is incomplete without a properly working compass. Poor visibility due to weather or terrain can disorient backcountry users, and a compass is the best way to regain one's bearings. Once again, this piece of equipment is useless without the proper knowledge of its use. Avoid cheap models—a flawed compass is worse than none at all.

MAPS

Maps are provided for the trips in this guide, produced from reduced copies of 7.5-minute USGS quadrangles. The first number following the "Map" heading in the individual trip descriptions refers to the corresponding map for each route.

TOPOGRAPHIC MAPS

Most major outdoor retailers no longer carry USGS maps per se, opting for kiosks that print custom made topographic maps instead. Below is a listing of the USGS 7.5-minute topographic maps with corresponding snowshoe trip numbers. The United States Geological Survey produces the 7.5-minute quadrangles, the finest maps to be found. Perfectly suited for recreational use, these maps show physical features and contours. Snowshoers venturing into the backcountry should always carry the appropriate "topo" maps for the particular area in which they will be traveling. State indexes can be ordered from the government at (800) USA-MAPS or (800) HELP-MAP, or by writing to:

USGS Information Services
Box 25286
Denver, CO 80225

With the appropriate state and map names, you can order directly from the Customer Service department of the USGS at (800) 435-7627. In 2005 maps were selling for $6.00 apiece, plus a small handling charge per order. The USGS accepts VISA or MasterCard for payment.

Many outdoor retailers also carry USGS maps. Below you will find a listing of these maps for the Lake Tahoe region with corresponding snowshoe trip numbers.

MAP NAME	TRIP NUMBERS
1 Cisco Grove	5
2 Soda Springs	5, 6
3 Norden	7, 8, 9, 10, 11, 12, 13, 14, 15
4 Truckee	14, 15
5 Martis Peak	16, 17
6 Mt. Rose	18, 19, 20, 21, 22, 23, 24, 25, 26
7 Washoe City	18
8 Granite Chief	1, 3
9 Tahoe City	1, 2. 3, 4, 65
11 Marlette Lake	27
12 Homewood	57, 58, 59, 60, 61, 62, 63, 64
13 Meeks Bay	57, 58, 59, 60, 61, 62
14 Glenbrook	27, 28, 30
15 Emerald Bay	54, 55, 56
16 South Lake Tahoe	29
17 Echo Lake	31, 32, 33, 46, 50, 51, 52, 53, 54
18 Freel Peak	30, 31, 32, 33, 34, 35, 36, 37, 39, 40, 41, 42, 46
19 Caples Lake	33, 44, 45, 46, 47, 48, 49
20 Carson Pass	43, 44, 45, 46, 47, 48
21 Markleeville	38

COMPUTER SOFTWARE

As we move further into the computer age, software companies have developed computer programs utilizing the USGS maps as a base. Some of these programs are better than others, including a variety of options that the user can access to customize maps for personal use. With a decent desktop color printer, you can produce maps that rival the quality of the USGS ones, albeit not on the same-size sheet of paper. The cost of a typical program equals the cost of 15 maps, which makes the idea of paying for the software somewhat appealing if you plan on purchasing many maps. Your local backpacking store is typically the best source for purchasing these programs. In the near future you will be able to buy computer disks directly from the USGS containing a specified selection and number of topo maps per disk.

FOREST SERVICE MAPS

The U.S. Forest Service produces a number of good maps that are well-suited for general purposes but, as a rule, should not be substituted for the more accurate USGS maps. These small-scale maps are sometimes helpful for

Index of USGS Maps

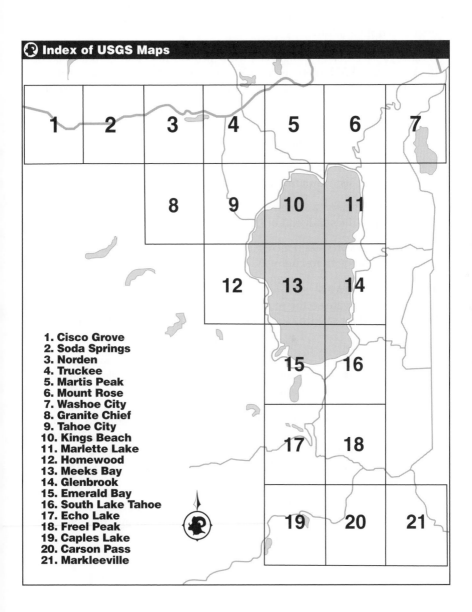

1. Cisco Grove
2. Soda Springs
3. Norden
4. Truckee
5. Martis Peak
6. Mount Rose
7. Washoe City
8. Granite Chief
9. Tahoe City
10. Kings Beach
11. Marlette Lake
12. Homewood
13. Meeks Bay
14. Glenbrook
15. Emerald Bay
16. South Lake Tahoe
17. Echo Lake
18. Freel Peak
19. Caples Lake
20. Carson Pass
21. Markleeville

determining highway routes to trailheads or for gaining a wider perspective of the territory. You can purchase these at the appropriate Forest Service Ranger Station. A list of maps covering the greater Lake Tahoe region and a brief description follows:

A Guide to the Desolation Wilderness—a 2 inch = 1 mile topographic map of the Desolation Wilderness area. This is a very accurate map that could be substituted for the corresponding USGS maps for trails within the Wilderness.

Eldorado National Forest—a ½ inch = 1 mile map covering an area from the middle of Lake Tahoe south to Ebbetts Pass.

Lake Tahoe Basin Management Unit—a ½ inch = 1 mile map showing the immediate lands surrounding Lake Tahoe.

Tahoe National Forest—a ½ inch = 1 mile map showing forest lands south of Highway 70 to the south end of Lake Tahoe and west toward Nevada City.

Toiyabe National Forest—a ½ inch = 1 mile map of the forest lands on the east side of Lake Tahoe from Highway 70 to the south end of the lake.

ADDITIONAL MAPS

At least two private-sector recreation maps of the Lake Tahoe area have been produced for sale from outdoor retailers. They can be used as excellent reference maps.

North Lake Tahoe Basin & South Lake Tahoe Basin—this pair of multi-colored, relief-shaded maps cover the greater Lake Tahoe area at a scale of 1 inch = 1 mile. Complete with contours, these maps show recreational trails and roads, primarily for summertime users, including hikers, mountain bikers and 4WD users. Both maps combined cover a wide area around the lake, including all of the snowshoe trails described in this book. Published by Fine Edge Productions, they sell for $8.95 apiece. As good as these maps are, they still are no substitute for the USGS topo maps.

Recreation Map of Lake Tahoe—a high quality publication, this map covers the recreation land immediately surrounding the lake. Multi-colored, relief-shaded and including contours, this map also makes for an excellent reference tool showing the network of hiking trails around Lake Tahoe.

EQUIPMENT CHECKLIST

GEAR

snowshoes
ski poles/avalanche probes
pack
10 essentials:
    maps
    compass
    flashlight or headlamp (extra batteries & bulb)
    knife
    extra food
    extra clothing
    sunglasses & sunscreen
    matches (in waterproof container)
    candles (or firestarter)
    first aid/emergency kit
toilet paper
repair kit: cord, tape, safety pins, etc.
water bottles or thermos (filled)
signaling devices: whistle and mirror
safety equipment:
    avalanche cord
    avalanche detectors
    snow shovel
    cellular phone

OPTIONAL GEAR

camera
binoculars
GPS receiver

CLOTHING

winter boots
gaiters
socks (liners & outer socks)
shell parka (Gore-Tex or equivalent)
shell pants (Gore-Tex or equivalent)
jacket
vest
shirt
gloves or mitts
hats (for sun & cold)
underwear
pants

Route to Snow Valley Peak (Trip 27)

CHAPTER 4

How to Use This Guide

This guidebook is designed specifically for snowshoers desiring opportunities for one-day trips into the Tahoe-Sierra, an area centered around Lake Tahoe and roughly delineated by Interstate 80 on the north and California Highway 88 on the south. An attempt has been made not to simply tailor existing cross-country ski routes for snowshoe trips, but to identify areas that are specifically well suited for snowshoeing, although some trips will indeed correspond to known cross-country routes in some areas.

Half of the trips described in this guide are classified as suited for snowshoers of moderate abilities, 32% for beginners and 18% for the more experienced. These ratings are subjective and prone to the random conditions of nature. A difficult trip could easily be accomplished on a day when the weather is clear and the snow conditions perfect, while a half-mile trip rated as easy could turn into a desperate struggle for snowshoers wading through 5 feet of fresh powder while a driving wind knocks them to and fro.

The intention of the author is that this guide will provide enough information to direct readers to the trailhead, to a destination, and back again, but not so much as to require lots of reading while on the trail. After all, the backcountry was meant to be enjoyed first-hand.

Duration: This information is a subjective evaluation of how much of a typical winter's day should be set aside for the complete enjoyment of a particular trip. Surely, there will be those who can complete trips in less time than is listed, just as others may feel hurried. Hopefully, the average snowshoer will find these estimates reasonable.

Distance: Distances have been accurately determined in the field using the 7.5-minute USGS quadrangles. Since exact routes are difficult to duplicate on the ever-changing winter landscape, there may be some slight discrepancies in distance from time to time, but certainly nothing dramatic.

Difficulty: For the purpose of this guide, difficulty ratings have been grouped into four categories: easy, moderate, difficult, and extreme. Easy trips should be well suited to beginning snowshoers as the terrain is gentle, the trips are relatively short, and the routefinding is minimal. Moderate trips pass over more complex terrain, are typically longer, and require some routefinding skills to successfully negotiate. Trips that receive a difficult rating move the snowshoer across steeper terrain, cover greater distances, and may necessitate considerable routefinding skill. These journeys may present more objective dangers as well, such as avalanche potential, or a greater possibility of exposure to inclement weather. The last rating, extreme, is for those trips that push the limits of technical skill, endurance, and vulnerability to the forces of nature. These journeys are for experienced snowshoers who are technically proficient, in good condition, and well qualified to evaluate potential hazards.

Elevation: The first four-digit entry under this heading is for the trailhead elevation at the start of a trip. The second number is the elevation at the high point of round trips, except in cases where the farthest destination is substantially lower than the highest point en route. For these trips, three elevations (starting, high point, and ending) are listed. For the few one-way trips that require a shuttle, three elevations are listed: the beginning trailhead, the high point and the ending trailhead.

Maps: Here you will find the names of the corresponding 7.5-minute quadrangles covering the area of the trip.

Introduction: The introduction gives a brief picture of the highlights of that particular journey.

How to get there: Clear instructions are given for getting to the trailhead.

Description: The trip description gives directions for getting around the backcountry in an orderly fashion. The intent is to avoid an overly detailed discourse so that you can enjoy the backcountry experience without continual dependence on a book.

FYI: Under the "For Your Information" heading, you will find additional matters of importance.

Warm-ups: Many winter enthusiasts find a trip to the winter backcountry incomplete without sitting by the fire sipping their favorite brew after an exhilarating romp through the snow. For those who enjoy a hot drink or a warm meal following a snowshoe trip, you will find some suggestions for accentuating your experience. A completely subjective and random formula was used in evaluating these establishments. They had to in some way capture certain undefinable elements related to an outdoor ambiance, as well as provide decent food or drink at a reasonable cost. Other intangibles were considered, not the least of which was whether the staff was reasonably friendly to poorly dressed, unshaven, perspiration-soaked, snow-sodden customers.

TRIP TABLE

EASY TRIPS:

Trip	Duration	Distance	Elevation
9. Peter Grubb Hut & Round Valley	½ Day	5.25	7200/7900
10. Castle Valley Loop	½ Day	3.75	7200/7795
14. Donner Memorial State Park	½ Day	2.5	5935/5975
19. Tamarack Lake	½ Day	1.0	8615/8835
22. Tahoe Meadows	½ Day	Varies	8550
23. Chickadee Ridge	½ Day	3.0	8550/9225
24. Upper Galena Creek	½ Day	6.0	8835/9200
26. Mt. Rose Hwy. to Lake Vista	½ Day	1.75	8150/8430
28. Spooner Lake	½ Day	2.0	7000
31. Big Meadow	½ Day	1.75	7250/7550
34. Grass Lake Meadow	½ Day	Varies	7700
38. Grover Hot Springs State Park	½ Day	3.0	5825/6000
40. Hope Valley	½ Day	Varies	7080
41. Scotts Lake	½ Day	3.0	7115/8035
50. Echo Lakes	½ Day	Varies	7320/7525
54. Angora Lookout	½ Day	3.75	6670/7285
55. Fallen Leaf Lake	½ to Full Day	Varies	6300/6550
57. Meeks Creek	½ Day	3.5	6240/6350
58. Sugar Pine Point State Park	½ Day	Varies	6300
59. General Creek	½ Day	Varies	6320
63. Blackwood Canyon	½ Day	Varies	6230
65. Page Meadow	½ Day	3.0	6975/6925

MODERATE TRIPS:

Trip	Duration	Distance	Elevation
1. Pole Creek & Bradley Hut	Full Day	10.25	6020/7610
3. Alpine Meadows to Five Lakes	½ Day	3.25	6560/7500
4. Tahoe City to Peak 9572	½ to ¾ Day	5.0	6320/7572
5. Loch Leven Lakes	¾ Day	5.0	5790/6900
6. Matrimony Ridge Vista	¾ Day	5.5	6050/6895
7. Donner Peak & Mt. Judah	½ Day	4.5	7090/8243
8. Donner Pass Lakes & Boreal Ridge Loop	½ Day	3.25	7200/7445
12. Andesite Peak	½ Day	3.5	7200/8219
13. Summit Lake	½ Day	4.25	7200/7475
16. Brockway Summit to Peak 7766	½ Day	1.25	7000/8742
17. Martis Peak	¾ Day	8.0	7000/8742
18. Galena Creek (lower route)	¾ Day	4.25	6775/8640
25. Relay Peak	¾ Day	9.0	8835/10338
29. Castle Rock	½ Day	2.5	7800/7550/7900
30. High Meadows	½ Day	6.5	6526/7775
32. Big Meadow to Scotts Lake & Hwy. 88	¾ Day	4.25	7250/8080
33. Big Meadow to Round Lake	¾ Day	5.25	7275/8050
36. Horse Meadow	¾ Day	8.5	7480/8520
39. Hope Valley Overlook	¾ Day	6.0	6900/8100
43. Crater Lake	½ Day	2.75	7360/8595
44. Red Lake Peak	½ Day	5.0	8560/10063
45. Meiss Lake	¾ Day	7.0	8560/8315
47. Little Round Top	Full Day	10.25	8560/9590
48. Winnemucca & Round Top Lakes	¾ Day	6.0	8600/9415
49. Emigrant Lake	¾ Day	8.25	7685/8600
51. Becker Peak	½ Day	3.25	7320/8325
52. Echo Peak	Full Day	9.25	7320/8895
54. Angora Lakes	½ Day	6.75	6670/7450
59. General Creek	¾ to Full Day	Varies	6320/7700
60. McKinney, Lily & Miller Lakes & Miller Meadow	½ to ¾ Day	Varies	6320/7100

MODERATE TRIPS (continued)**:**

Trip	Duration	Distance	Elevation
61.Richardson Lake & Ludlow Hut	Full Day	13.75	6320/7445
62. Buck Lake	¾ Day	9.5	6320/7550
64. Stanford Rock	¾ Day	6.5	6320/8473

DIFFICULT TRIPS:

Trip	Duration	Distance	Elevation
2. Silver Peak	Full Day	9.75	6020/8424
11. Castle Peak	¾ Day	6.25	7200/9103
15. Donner Lake- Shallenberger Ridge Loop	Full Day	9.75	5935/7469
20. Slide Mountain	½ Day	2.0	8900/9680
21. Mt. Rose	Full Day	10.0	8900/10776
27. Snow Valley Peak	Full Day	9.5	7145/9214
30. Star Lake	Full Day	11.0	6525/9125
42. Waterhouse Peak	¾ Day	5.0	7115/9497
46. Carson Pass to Big Meadows & Highway 89	Full Day	7.5	8560/8795/7250
53. Ralston Peak	¾ Day	5.0	6530/9235

EXTREME TRIPS:

Trip	Duration	Distance	Elevation
35. Thompson Peak	½ Day	1.5	7730/9340
37. Freel Peak	Full Day	11.5	7480/10881
48. Round Top	Full Day	Varies	8600/10381
56. Mt. Tallac	Full Day	4.5	6530/9735

Donner Lake from Donner Peak (Trip 7)

CHAPTER 5

North Tahoe

The concrete ribbon of Interstate 80 provides indirect access to Lake Tahoe for the bulk of travelers headed to one of America's favorite winter playgrounds. Only fitting is the fact that many trips into the Tahoe backcountry are served by the same road. From I-80, three major highways radiate into the basin on the north side of the lake, granting entry to trailheads. While the south side of the lake offers mountain grandeur, the west side quiet serenity, and the east side undeveloped isolation, the north side combines elements of all three. A wide variety of scenery and experiences await the snowshoer in the north part of the Lake Tahoe backcountry.

Donner Summit is perhaps the easiest trans-Sierra pass in northern California to access. The four-lane highway remains open all winter, except in the very worst of conditions. A number of snowshoe trips begin at or near Donner Summit and Donner Pass, the high point of the old two-lane road that was replaced by the four-lane freeway. With elevations over 7,000 feet, both passes attain altitudes sufficient to provide recreationists with an adequate supply of snow for a considerable season of use. Subalpine lakes, lofty summits and beautiful vistas are here in abundance.

In addition to I-80, California Highways 89 and 267 and Nevada State Route 431 provide additional access to other snowshoe trips in the north section. Several trips radiate from the Mt. Rose Highway, which crests at the highest all-year pass in the Sierra at 8,933 feet. Trips starting from the other two roads offer spectacular scenery and superb views.

Not only does the north Tahoe region offer visitors a wide range of scenery, but also plenty of trips for snowshoers of every skill level and experience.

Although the north end of Lake Tahoe has seen significant development, the area does not seem to be as crowded as the south end. Nonetheless, a significant population of year-around residents, coupled with an influx of winter tourists, creates a mass of humanity on a sunny winter weekend. Timing your departure to avoid the late afternoon crush of vehicles leaving the area's ski resorts is an extremely prudent move. And even though there are a lot of folks congregating at the north end of the lake, with a little care toward the selection of your trip you should be able to leave most of the crowds behind.

Major towns at this end of the lake providing amenities for tourists include Truckee, Tahoe City, and Incline Village.

Route to Mt. Rose

TRIP **1**

Pole Creek & Bradley Hut

see map
on page
40

Duration: Full day
Distance: 10.25 miles round trip
Difficulty: Moderate
Elevation: 6020/7610
Maps: *Tahoe City & Granite Chief* 7.5' quadrangles

Introduction: Harold T. Bradley was a university professor and former president of the Sierra Club who, after experiencing the pleasures of the hut system in the Swiss Alps, proposed a similar string of six alpine huts that would span the mountains above Lake Tahoe from Donner to Echo Summit. Only four of the huts were ever realized, the last completed in 1957 within the Five Lakes Basin, directly above what would one day become the Alpine Meadows Ski Area. This final hut was named as a memorial to Harold's late wife Josephine.

In 1984 the inclusion of the Five Lakes Basin within the designated Granite Chief Wilderness created a profound dilemma for the Bradley Hut. Since legal wilderness is defined as "an area without permanent improvements or human habitation," the existence of the structure was incompatible with wilderness. After much debate, rather than destroy the hut, a plan was worked out to move the structure to the current location along Pole Creek. With the aid of many volunteers, the structure was relocated, refurbished, and reopened for the winter of 1998. Today visitors can follow the record of the original construction as well as the eventual relocation through the photographs mounted on the walls in the hut.

The trip to Bradley Hut is a pleasant experience, even for those not anticipating an overnight stay. Following the moderate grade of a snow-covered road, travelers weave their way through light forest for the first 2 miles and then follow the banks of Pole Creek for another 3 miles up into the scenic basin at the head of the canyon. Along the way there are stunning

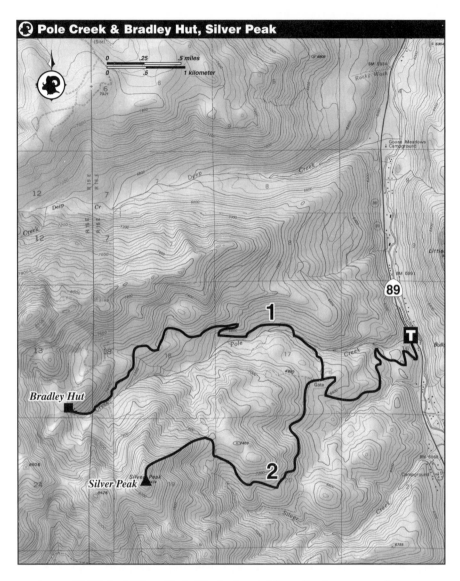

views of 8424-foot Silver Peak. The hut provides a fine base camp for snowshoers and skiers who want to explore the sloping terrain above the creek or the backcountry beyond. Overnighters must arrange for use of the Bradley Hut (see FYI).

How to get there: Travel south on California Highway 89, 5.9 miles from the junction with Interstate 80 in Truckee, to a small plowed area on the west side of the roadway. This parking area is just south of Pole Creek, diagonally across the highway from a contemporary wooden structure signed OLSON CONST CO. Park judiciously in the limited area. From the clearing you should be able to see the beginning of the snow-covered road, Forest Road 08, paralleling the highway as it heads into the trees.

Description: Follow the road as it winds and climbs away from the highway through moderate forest. If you feel comfortable leaving the security of the established route, you can save some distance by heading directly cross-country rather than following the circuitous path of the road. As the mild climb along the road progresses, you have nice views of the surrounding hills and eventually of Silver Peak itself.

After 1.75 miles, you reach a junction with another road to the left, which heads toward Silver Peak (see Trip 2). From the junction, take the right-hand road north on a moderate descent into the drainage of Pole

Bradley Hut

Creek. After you draw near to the stream, proceed up the road on a gentle climb to a wooden bridge. You cross the bridge and begin a moderate climb above the north bank of Pole Creek through widely scattered ponderosa pines. As you continue, the summit of Silver Peak peeks above the tops of the trees to the southwest.

At 3 miles from the trailhead, you begin to climb more steeply as the road switchbacks up the hillside. In another 0.25 mile you reach a junction, where you should follow FS Road 08 as it bends sharply back to the left, heading west again. On the steady ascent, the stately form of Silver Peak makes regular appearances over the next mile above a widely scattered forest. After you cross a feeder creek, work your way over to the main channel of Pole Creek, and follow alongside the stream toward the upper basin. Just past the 5-mile mark you find the relocated Bradley Hut near the road on the fringe of the open terrain at the head of the canyon.

The two-story, A-frame cabin with matching outhouse provides temporary shelter for day-trippers. When visiting the cabin observe the posted rules and do your part to insure that this historic legacy will remain intact for generations to come.

FYI: For overnight reservations, or for more information about the Bradley Hut, contact the Sierra Club at:

Clair Tappaan Lodge
P.O. Box 36
Norden, CA 95724
(530) 426-3632

Warm-ups: When the "PIZ" fell off the sign out front, the owner seized the moment and renamed the restaurant ZA's. This momentous occasion aside, great Italian food served at reasonable prices probably has more to do with the overwhelming success of this restaurant than the offbeat name. Space is limited, so you may have to wait for a table, but you won't be disappointed in the food when it comes, or the size of the check, for that matter. Lunch is served from 11 A.M. to 3 P.M. and dinner from 4:30 P.M. till closing. Za's is located in Tahoe City at 395 North Lake Blvd. (Hwy. 28), across from the fire station.

T R I P **2**

Silver Peak

Duration: Full day
Distance: 9.75 miles round trip
Difficulty: Difficult
Elevation: 6020/8424
Map: *Tahoe City* 7.5' quadrangle

Introduction: During sunny weather, Silver Peak provides one of the best lake views in the entire Tahoe basin. Most of the trip follows an easy grade along a snow-covered road, but the last 0.75 mile gains 1000 feet up a steep ridge to the top and should be attempted only by experienced parties. The lofty summit is quite airy and wind-prone, at times having some less than ideal snow conditions. If you don't mind the challenge of high-angle slopes and wind-blasted aeries, Silver Peak rewards you with an unsurpassed vista. Experiencing the awesome view upon reaching the summit on a sunny, windless day creates an idyllic memory.

How to get there: Travel south on California Highway 89, 5.9 miles from the junction with Interstate 80 in Truckee, to a small plowed area on the west side of the roadway. This parking area is just south of Pole Creek, diagonally across the highway from a contemporary wooden structure signed OLSON CONST CO. Park judiciously in the limited area. From the clearing you should be able to see the beginning of the snow-covered road, Forest Road 08, paralleling the highway as it heads into the trees.

Description: Follow the road as it winds and climbs away from the highway through moderate forest. If you feel comfortable leaving the security of the established route, you can save some distance by heading directly cross-country rather than following the circuitous path of the road. As the mild climb along the road progresses, you have nice views of the surrounding hills and eventually of Silver Peak itself.

After 1.75 miles, you reach a junction with another road to the right, which heads downhill toward Pole Creek (see Trip 1). Bear left at this junction and continue to follow your road south as it climbs through a mixed forest of pine, fir, and occasional cedar. If you want to forgo the road, you can take a more direct course straight over Peak 7403 to the northeast ridge of Silver Peak. Otherwise, remain on the road as it circles the hillside on a mild grade, reaching an overlook just shy of 3 miles from the trailhead. From this vantage point, you can gaze southeast across the waters of Lake Tahoe to Freel Peak, the highest mountain in the Tahoe basin. Another 0.75 mile of snowshoeing along the road brings you to the northeast ridge of Silver Peak, 3.75 miles from the trailhead.

Now you leave the gentle grade of the road behind and climb much more steeply up the ridge. As you gain elevation, follow a direct line southwest up the ridge to the summit, except for a pair of rock outcroppings which should be passed on the right. The final pitch just below the summit is fairly steep and may be composed of wind-packed snow, so some parties may wish to bring ice axes and crampons during periods of extremely hard snow conditions.

The view from the summit of Silver Peak is spectacular. Lake Tahoe is revealed in all its glory, and the basin's highest peaks provide the perfect backdrop. Thousands of feet below, the busyness of Squaw Valley stands in stark contrast to the remoteness at the summit. You can while away the hours watching brightly-clad skiers descending the numerous runs of one of Tahoe's largest resorts.

FYI: Under stable conditions, experienced skiers and snowboarders may want to pack along their gear—the descent of Silver Peak provides outstanding backcountry possibilities.

Warm-ups: For an unbeatable start to the day, try one of the many omelettes at The Squeeze Inn, on Main Street (10060 Donner Pass Road) in the quaint town of Truckee. The Squeeze Inn opens at 7 A.M. and closes at 2 P.M. Call (530) 587-9814 for more information.

Lake Tahoe from Silver Peak

TRIP **3**

Alpine Meadows to Five Lakes

Duration: One-half day
Distance: 3.25 miles round trip
Difficulty: Moderate to difficult
Elevation: 6560/7500
Maps: *Tahoe City & Granite Chief* 7.5′ quadrangles

see map on page 46

Introduction: A short but strenuous climb leads to a quiet basin harboring five small lakes. An extremely popular summer destination, the Five Lakes area is seldom seen during the winter months. On a typical winter day, hundreds if not thousands of skiers cavort along nearby ridges and slopes at the upper limits of Alpine Meadows and Squaw Valley ski resorts, but the Five Lakes region remains relatively untouched. From Alpine Meadows, a route across the steep mountainside past impassable-looking cliffs and over to the lakes would seem inconceivable, but a route does exist for those who don't mind the steep ascent. Due to the precipitous slopes one must cross and the potential for avalanche, this trip should be attempted only when snow conditions are stable. The high, open terrain provides bird's-eye views of Alpine Meadows during the ascent.

How to get there: Travel south on California Highway 89, 9.5 miles from the junction with Interstate 80 in Truckee, to the access road for Alpine Meadows. Travel up Alpine Meadows Road 2.1 miles to the second of two intersections both marked DEER PARK ROAD. Parking is extremely limited, so try to find a place in a plowed area near this intersection. If parking near the trailhead is impossible, you may have to park in the ski-area parking lot and bum a ride back from an agreeable skier.

Description: Climb up the bank on the north side of the road and begin the moderately steep, continuous ascent across the south-facing hillside through a light covering of fir and pine. A quick visual inspection should

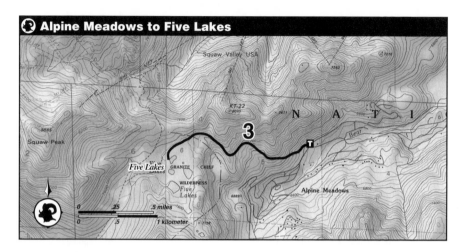

reveal that this is not a route to be tried in unstable circumstances—this slope could be prone to avalanches under certain conditions, and nasty cornices loom above you at the top of the ridge. As you gain elevation, pleasant views of Alpine Meadows should calm your spirits as the trees begin to thin. During calm weather, this slope is marked by myriad ski and snowboard tracks, which might further allay any apprehension about the stability of the slope.

Continue the diagonal ascent across the north side of the canyon until you reach a broad gully. Make an angling traverse around the head of this gully and then cross the ridge at the most convenient spot, avoiding the rock

Descending from Five Lakes Basin

cliffs. From the ridge, steady progress brings you to another canyon, where you should turn northwest and climb to its head. Ascend to the low point and then bear south as you travel over gentler terrain beyond the lip of the canyon. A short, gentle ascent brings you to the first of the Five Lakes. The relatively level basin provides easy terrain for exploration of the other lakes.

FYI: Consult the avalanche report before your trip (see Appendix I for the phone number). Accurate backcountry information may be hard to come by at the ski area—your best bet may be the guys in the repair shop.

Warm-ups: At the intersection of Highway 89 and Alpine Meadows Road sits the historic River Ranch Lodge. Combining a roaring fireplace with a great view and excellent food, the restaurant/bar provides the perfect place for a wonderful evening. Disheveled snowshoers will feel right at home dining with the ski crowd despite the upscale dining and moderately expensive prices (entrees range from $16.95 to $32.95). Follow a delicious appetizer of Seared Sesame Coated Ahi Tuna with creatively prepared poultry, seafood, and game dishes, including roasted fresh elk loin and wild salmon. You can check out a menu at **www.riverranchlodge.com** or phone (530) 583-4264 or (800) 535-9900 for more information.

TRIP 4

Tahoe City to Peak 7572

Duration: One-half to three-quarter day
Distance: 5 miles round trip
Difficulty: Moderate to difficult
Elevation: 6320/7572
Map: *Tahoe City* 7.5′ quadrangle

see map on page 48

Introduction: For those snowshoers who don't mind a nearly continuous climb with occasional steep sections, the trip from Tahoe City to Peak 7572 at the east end of the Cinder Cone provides supreme views of Lake Tahoe and the surrounding mountains. Nearly the entire surface of the lake is seen from this northern vantage point, along with several ski areas, lakeshore communities, and noteworthy peaks scattered around the basin.

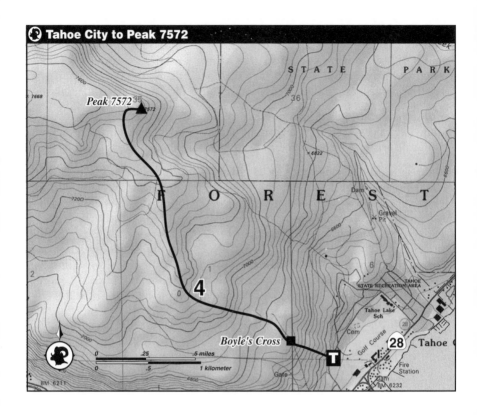

The steepest part of the climb is the initial 0.25-mile section from the parking area, which leads to an open hillside with a fine lake view and a large wooden cross rising above the snow—a memorial to a colorful former resident of Tahoe City. Most of the route passes through a light forest that inhibits views of the surrounding terrain until the stunning climax of the trip atop the peak. However, along the way there are brief views of Tahoe and the peaks above the Squaw Valley and Alpine Meadows ski areas. Snowmobiles may be seen and heard in this area, with the most likely encounters occurring near a crossing of the Fiberboard Freeway, a major snowmobile route between Brockway Summit and Tahoe City, 1.75 miles into the trip.

How to get there: From the Y-intersection with Highway 28 in Tahoe City, travel northbound on Highway 89 for 0.2 miles and turn right just past a Chevron gas station onto Fairway Drive. Follow Fairway Drive another 0.2 mile to the Fairway Community Center on the right. Park in the lot as space allows.

Description: From the community center, cross Fairway Drive and make a steep climb northwest up a hillside lightly covered by a mixed forest of Jeffrey pines, white firs, sugar pines and incense cedars. After 0.25 mile the terrain eases considerably and an old wooden cross can be seen protruding out of the snow. The memorial was placed sometime after Tahoe City resident William Boyle was buried here on February 12, 1912. Legend has it that Boyle requested his drinking buddies bury him on the hill so he could continue to keep an eye on them. The location is a fine site for a memorial, as the cross is backdropped very nicely by a view of Lake Tahoe.

Shortly beyond the cross you pass beneath some power lines and emerge from the forest into a pair of clearings. Beyond the second clearing, you return to the forest and climb moderately up the slope for a short while until the grade eases to more of a mild ascent.

At 1.2 miles the route veers north to follow a more defined ridge, where the trees part occasionally to offer views to the west of the topography around the Alpine Meadows and Squaw Valley ski areas. Continue along the ridge to the crossing of the Fiberboard Freeway, 1.75 miles from the parking lot. In summer the road is a sedan-worthy route that is very popular with the mountain bike crowd as well. In winter the road is well traveled

Snowshoer near Boyle's Cross above Tahoe City

by snowmobiles also, as evidenced by the preponderance of tracks you will usually see here.

Beyond the road crossing you climb the ridge northwest and then north toward Peak 7572. Nearing the top you curve east to arrive at an open, rocky aerie that offers an excellent view of Lake Tahoe. Thanks to the exposure, you should be able to find a snow-free rock upon which to sit and enjoy the scenery. Nearly the entire lake springs into view, rimmed by myriad snow-covered peaks. Numerous Tahoe landmarks are visible from this vantage point—remember to pack along a map large enough to help identify them.

FYI: Although snowmobiles are allowed into this area, you can minimize your chances of an encounter by planning your trip for a weekday. The chance of meeting snowmobilers is highest near the Fiberboard Freeway, 1.75 miles from the trailhead, a popular snowmobile route between Brockway Summit and Tahoe City.

Warm-ups: The Fire Sign Café in Tahoe City has been a local hot spot since 1970. The restaurant is extremely busy on weekends but the freshly prepared dishes are worth the wait. Not only will you find breakfast fare like bacon and eggs, but more exotic fare such as Cape Cod Benedict and dill and artichoke omelette. Lunch, served until 3 P.M., is also available, but breakfast remains the main attraction. The restaurant occupies an old home at 1785 W. Lake Boulevard, 2 miles south of the center of town. To avoid the long weekend wait, time your arrival for the 7 A.M. opening. Call (530) 583-0871 for more information.

TRIP **5**

Loch Leven Lakes

see map
on page
52

Duration: Three-quarter day
Distance: 5 miles round trip
Difficulty: Moderate
Elevation: 5790/6900
Maps: *Cisco Grove & Soda Springs* 7.5′ quadrangles

Introduction: Described in an early edition of Jeffrey Schaffer's classic guide *The Tahoe Sierra* as "probably the best constructed trail in the Tahoe Sierra," the path to Loch Leven Lakes is a very popular summertime trip for hikers. However, a winter excursion along the same route provides the antithesis to the summer experience. Although some cross-country skiers approach High Loch Leven Lake from the east via a marked trail, few winter enthusiasts accept the challenge of a snow trip following the route of the summer trail.

There are a couple of obstacles to surmount on the way to the lakes. First of all, during years of heavy snows, you may have to shovel some steps into the snowbank at the highway just to get started. In addition, you must cross the frequently traveled Southern Pacific Railroad tracks and face the same problem with the snowbank on the far side. This trip also requires some basic routefinding skills, but reaching the lakes is not particularly difficult.

Along with the solitude, snowshoers will find the Loch Leven Lakes to be quite scenic. Each of the three lakes possesses a unique charm. The open terrain near the beginning of the trip and around the lakes periodically provides fine views of the surrounding countryside.

How to get there: From Interstate 80, take the Big Bend exit (1.5 miles east of Cisco Grove and 6 miles west of the Soda Springs exit). From the exit ramp, follow old Highway 40 for 0.9 mile to the plowed parking area on the north side of the road. A Forest Service block building with a pit toilet is at the west end of the parking area.

Description: On a generally southward course, head directly up the moderately steep hillside amid scattered pines, firs, and cedars, attempting to

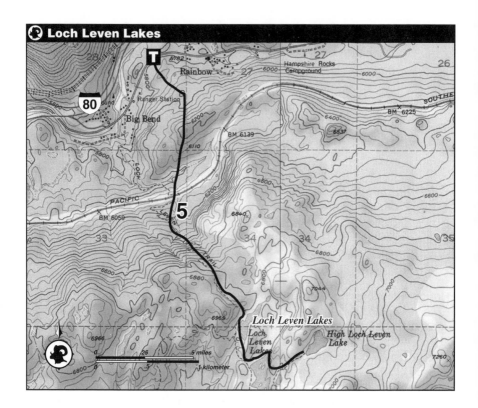

Loch Leven Lakes

anticipate a course that will result in the least amount of elevation loss on the far side. Beyond the top of the hill, you must descend into deeper forest and, 0.75 mile from the trailhead, cross a creek, which eventually feeds into the South Yuba River.

Past the creek, you begin climbing again, quickly reaching a double set of railroad tracks near a trestle. Keep an ear out for approaching trains—those chugging uphill are easily heard, but the ones descending from Donner Pass make far less noise and can sneak up on the unwary. If gaining the slope above the highway was difficult, you may have similar problems negotiating the snowbank on the far side of the tracks.

From the tracks, resume a moderately steep climb south through forest cover of pine and fir. Heading to the right of some bare cliffs, make a steady ascent southeast toward the top of the ridge. Near the crest you have nice views to the north of the Donner Summit area, thanks to a covering of lighter forest. For the next 0.5 mile you will find gentler territory between the top of the ridge and the first of the Loch Leven Lakes. Open, rolling terrain characterizes the area, the granite of summer softened considerably by the snows of winter. From the first lake proceed over a low hump, where you have fine views of the surrounding countryside, to the second and largest of the lakes. To reach High Loch Leven Lake you must travel another 0.25 mile, bearing east through a notch.

FYI: The location of the summer trailhead is shown incorrectly on the 1955 topo map—the trailhead was relocated 0.5 mile to the east, where the snowshoe description begins.

Warm-ups: There's only one restaurant near the trailhead. Fortunately, the Engadine Cafe in Rainbow Lodge happens to be that restaurant. Rivaling just about any fare the Lake Tahoe region has to offer, the cafe turns out wonderful meals with a touch of European flair for breakfast, lunch, and dinner. The wonderful food is complemented by the rustic but charming decor of the lodge. Since the lodge is owned and operated by Royal Gorge Cross-Country Ski Resort, you don't have to be concerned with whether the restaurant will be open during the winter months. The Sierra Cocktail Lounge and Bar is a great watering hole offering a light menu if you're not ravenous after your spin around the backcountry. You can sip a hot toddy by the mesmerizing fire or sample the history of the region while gazing at the black-and-white photographs lining the walls. If you're looking for a romantic weekend getaway, Rainbow Lodge offers fine bed-and-breakfast packages (2-night minimum; midweek rates). Reservations are recommended for dinner and Sunday brunch (530) 426-3661. For more information check out their website at **www.royalgorge.com**. Rainbow Lodge is located at 50800 Hampshire Rocks Road, 0.5 mile west of the Big Bend Exit. If Hampshire Rocks Road is in good shape, simply drive 2.5 miles east from the trailhead to Rainbow Lodge. If not, take I-80 from Cisco Grove to the Big Bend Exit and double back 0.5 mile to the west.

Old pine near Loch Leven Lakes

Matrimony Ridge Vista

Duration: Three-quarter day
Distance: 5.5 miles round trip
Difficulty: Moderate
Elevation: 6050/6895
Map: *Soda Springs* 7.5' quadrangle

see map
on page
55

Introduction: The usual superlatives one attributes to inspiring views seem inadequate when applied to the vista found at the destination of this trip. The 360° panorama includes northern Sierra landmarks almost too numerous to mention. Bravely clinging to the tenuous soil near the end of an exposed ridge, a weather-beaten Jeffrey pine picturesquely frames the craggy profile of Devils Peak. Beneath the canopy of its overhanging branches at least one couple has taken the vows of marriage, and ever since, the conifer has been known to an ever-expanding group of locals as Matrimony Tree. Even if nuptials are not on your itinerary, the site promises a celebratory experience marrying the modest effort required to reach the tree with a truly stunning vista.

Even so, the 2.75-mile excursion up to this reward is not entirely a bouquet of roses. Although much of the trip passes through sparsely forested terrain and some of the route is marked, you will have to use your routefinding skills to reach Matrimony Tree. In addition, the route intersects the Southern Pacific railroad tracks 0.75 mile from the trailhead, necessitating that you exercise caution when crossing the twin set of tracks, paying particular attention to avoiding the less noisy trains gliding down from Donner Pass. In years of decent snowfall, chances are you will also have to cut steps in order to ascend the far bank above the tracks (don't forget your snow shovel). These cautions aside, experienced snowshoers can successfully consummate their journey to Matrimony Tree with a modicum of effort.

Trailhead: Leave Interstate 80 at the Kingvale exit and follow Donner Pass Road west 0.6 mile to an underpass, which is 0.1 mile beyond Donner Trail

Matrimony Ridge Vista

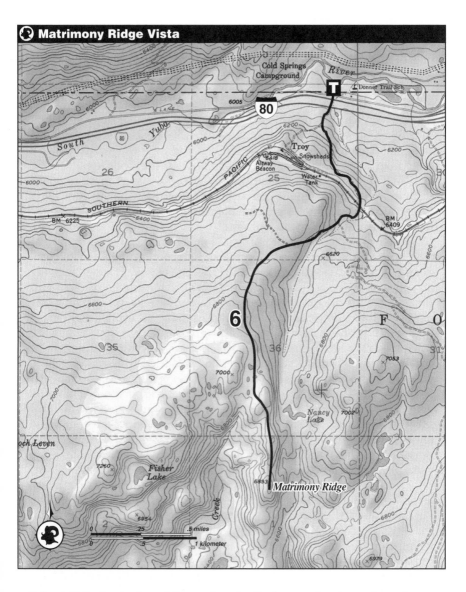

School. If the beginning of the road under the freeway has been plowed, you can park your vehicle there, otherwise parking is available on weekends back at the school.

Description: Begin your trip by traveling underneath both lanes of the freeway and then climb moderately up the snow-covered road to a Y-junction, 0.2 mile from Donner Pass Road. The junction is about 50 yards beyond an orange steel pole on your right. Turn left (south) and follow this road through scattered forest of pine and fir. You continue to climb at a moderate rate, eventually coming below the double set of railroad tracks at the 0.75-mile mark.

Carefully cross the tracks, keeping an ear out for approaching trains, particularly the muted sounds of those descending from Donner Pass. In normal snow years you will more than likely have to cut steps up the far bank where snowplows have created a steep wall of packed snow. Make the crossing upgrade from a trestle marked 1851 and 1853, where you will see a set of railroad crossing gates next to a small shed. The road crossing is also marked by orange poles on either side of the tracks. A short distance up the road you should see a blue-green sign reading: HIGH LOCH LEVEN LAKES NORDIC TRAIL. Beyond the sign, blue diamonds will help guide you up the road for the next part of your journey.

You travel up the road for nearly 0.25 mile from the railroad crossing, 1 mile from Donner Pass Road, to a marked junction. An obvious reddish-orange sign indicates you are about to cross one of Royal Gorge's network of cross-country ski trails. Nearby, a separate blue-green sign reads FOLLOW THE RAINBOW TRAIL 0.5 MI/0.8 KM. If you were to turn sharply uphill to the right for a very short distance you would encounter yet another sign, across from which is one more sign, reading TRAIL ONE WAY ONLY DOWNHILL, RAINBOW CONNECTION TO RAINBOW LODGE. If all of this seems confusing, you're absolutely right. The easiest way to proceed is to back up approximately 50 yards from the first set of signs. At this spot, look for a small, rectangular blue sign with white letters, which reads ERA NETWORK REALTY. A Y-junction with a lesser road angling uphill to your right is here—follow this road uphill and proceed. In a short distance you will intersect the convoluted route of quick twists and turns that the signs direct you to follow. Whoever came up with the signed route must have been intoxicated or must take perverse pleasure from having people stumble around like buffoons.

Once on the right track, you climb up this road for 0.25 mile to the broad, lightly forested crest of a ridge and another Y-junction. The route to the right is signed RAINBOW INTERCONNECT TO RAINBOW LODGE 6 KM, but you should proceed straight ahead on the left-hand route marked with every warning imaginable with the exception of "lions and tigers and bears." You continue up the road past a sign delineating your route as HIGH LOCH LEVEN LAKE BACKCOUNTRY TRAIL to where the grade eases. Here the route to Matrimony Ridge leaves the route to High Loch Leven Lake.

Leaving the path of the road, you now head toward the south climbing mildly on the east side of the ridge above a creek drainage. Soon the angle of ascent increases to moderately steep. As you climb, the trees begin to thin and the summit of Devils Peak appears to the east above the rise on the opposite side of the drainage below you. Proceed on a southerly course, continuing to skirt the east fringe of the crest, steadily climbing at a moderate rate. The more you climb the less the trees obstruct the increasingly dramatic views, until you reach the virtually bald zenith of the ridge and the incredible climax vista.

Perched at the apex of this unprotected ridge, the weather-beaten form of Matrimony Tree stands in rugged isolation, defying the frequently harsh conditions typical of such exposed promontories found at this elevation in the Sierra. The wind-sculptured, overhanging branches of this Jeffrey pine dramatically frame the rugged profile of Devils Peak, creating a picture-postcard view worthy of any mountain scenery calendar. Not to be outdone, additional snowcapped landforms demand your attention. The ridge delineating the upper boundary of Sugar Bowl Ski Area, which includes such noteworthy peaks as Crows Nest, Mt. Disney and Mt. Lincoln, reigns over the snow-covered terrain to the east beyond Devils Peak. Farther north, the white tips of Castle Peak, Basin Peak and Buzzard Roost pierce the winter sky. Directly south, the massive mound of Snow Mountain dominates the surrounding terrain, including the deep cleft of Royal Gorge, through which course the icy waters of the North Fork of the American River. On clear days, the vista extends beyond the western Sierra, across the Sacramento Valley and all the way to the coastal hills. Be sure to take along a large

Devils Peak from Ridge

enough map to help you identify some of the vast array of landmarks visible from this spot.

Once you've had your fill of the fantastic views, retrace your steps to the trailhead.

FYI: Snowboarders and backcountry skiers will love the nearly unlimited possibilities for cavorting down the surrounding slopes. A snowcamp combined with an extended period of fair weather would be the ideal conditions for an incomparable trip.

Warm-ups: The slogan for Shinneyboo Creek Cabins is "Luxury at the Threshold of the High Sierra," and with cast iron stoves, Jaccuzzi tubs, and queen-size beds with down comforters as standard accoutrements, the cozy cabins nestled into the Tahoe National Forest live up to the billing. Located north of Interstate 80 on Eagle Lakes Road (Exit 164), Shinneyboo Creek Cabins may be the ideal spot from where to venture out into the snowy backcountry by day and enjoy the creature comforts by night. Call (530) 587-5160 to check availability or make reservations, or do the same on the website at **www.shinneyboocreek.com**, where you can also view pictures of the cabins.

Snowshoer at Matrimony Tree

TRIP 7

Donner Peak & Mt. Judah

Duration: Full day
Distance: 4.5 miles round trip
Difficulty: Moderate
Elevation: 7090/8243
Map: *Norden* 7.5' quadrangle

see map on page 60

Introduction: Two peaks with superb views are the rewards of this trip. The distance is minimal, although the terrain is fairly steep, with the lone exception of the gentle, protracted crest leading to the summit of Mt. Judah. Although the hillsides are too steep for most cross-country skiers, you may encounter snowboarders and backcountry skiers careening down the north-facing slopes during periods of powder conditions. If you are an accomplished skier/snowboarder and you don't mind carrying the extra weight, such a descent might provide a reasonable, if not exhilarating, alternative to snowshoeing back to the car (avoid the slopes of Sugar Bowl Ski area).

How to get there: From Interstate 80, take the Soda Springs/Norden exit and travel 3.7 miles east on the old Donner Pass Road to the Alpine Skills International parking area at Donner Pass. You may park your vehicle in the lot for $5.00 per day. Check in at the front desk in the main building of ASI for a parking permit, which must be displayed on your dashboard to avoid having your vehicle towed.

Description: Begin snowshoeing south-southwest from the parking lot on a slight downhill grade until you reach a convenient spot from which to start up the moderately steep hillside of the northwest slope of Donner Peak. Proceed up the mountain through widely scattered conifers. As you climb, you have very nice views of Lake Van Norden to the west and the peaks of Donner Pass to the north. Before reaching the top of Donner Peak, you must climb over a minor summit, shown as Point 7696 on the *Norden* topo map.

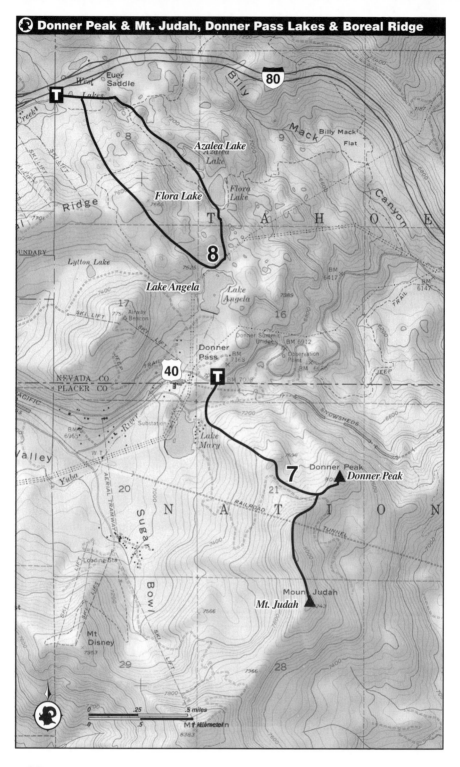

A fine vista is at this point, a foretaste of what is to come from the summit of Donner Peak. Continuing the climb, you pass through a stand of trees on the way to the saddle that separates Donner Peak and Mt. Judah.

Once at the saddle, turn northeast and make the short climb up moderate slopes to the summit rocks. From the top you have marvelous views in all directions. Donner Lake lies at your feet to the east, while massive cornices loom above along the ridge of Mt. Judah. An array of peaks spreads out both north and south.

From the summit, retrace your steps quickly back to the saddle between Mt. Judah and Donner Peak. If you were satisfied with the view from Donner Peak, you may elect to follow your trail back to the parking lot. Otherwise, from the saddle begin climbing steeply up the hillside toward the long summit ridge of Mt. Judah. Aim for a pair of reflectorized signs at the north edge of the ridge. Once on the crest the grade eases considerably as you head for the true summit at the south end. Remember to avoid the cornices along the west edge. Continue along the crest, dropping slightly before you make the last easy climb to the top.

The ridge and the summit of Mt. Judah offer a grand panorama of the north Tahoe countryside. A flurry of activity occurs to the north, including skiers and snowboarders on the ski slopes of Sugar Bowl and Donner Ski Ranch, trains chugging up the long grade toward Donner Pass, and hundreds of cars snaking along Interstate 80 headed for unknown points. The

Mt. Judah from near Donner Peak

bustling community of Truckee lies to the east beyond Donner Lake. A more remote scene is in the south, where myriad snow-covered peaks stretch along a series of ridges, beckoning the adventurous toward further exploration. For most people, the view from Mt. Judah is a perfect reward for a half-day's journey. After taking in the scenery, follow your steps back to the car.

FYI: If you find yourself at the summit of Mt. Judah with plenty of energy and time, you can accept the challenge of the more demanding route to Mt. Anderson along the ridge heading southeast from Mt. Lincoln. Be forewarned, this adds another 7 miles round trip to your journey.

Warm-ups: Alpine Skills International offers a reasonably priced bunk-and-breakfast package for anyone with their own sleeping bag and $25 (plus tax). For the serious outdoor enthusiast they also offer a wide variety of winter and summer backcountry programs. Call (530) 582-9170 or visit their website at **www.alpineskills.com.**

TRIP 8

Donner Pass Lakes & Boreal Ridge Loop

Duration: One-half day
Distance: 3.25 miles round trip
Difficulty: Moderate
Elevation: 7200/7445
Map: *Norden* 7.5′ quadrangle

see map
on page
60

Introduction: Aside from the potential routefinding problems, this trip would be rated easy, as the distance is short and the terrain is not particularly steep. However, the densely forested, undulating topography over the first mile can be somewhat confusing, requiring a modicum of navigational ability. For those willing to test their skills, the lakes offer pleasant scenery, and the view from the top of Boreal Ridge is splendid.

How to get there: Just west of Donner Summit take the Castle Peak exit from Interstate 80. Follow signs to the Sno-Park at the east end of the frontage road immediately south of the freeway.

Description: From the east end of the Sno-Park, head into medium forest cover and proceed for a little more than 0.25 mile on a course roughly paralleling the freeway. Near the edge of a clearing, turn southeast and head through somewhat convoluted terrain to a hillside 0.75 mile from the trailhead, from where you should be able to spot Azalea Lake. Descend to the lake, in a basin bounded by rock walls and steep hillsides. Flora Lake is directly south of Azalea through a narrow gap. Both lakes are quite picturesque, providing a serene setting for a rest stop or lunch.

From the second lake, climb south directly over a less wooded rise and descend to the north shore of Lake Angela, the largest of the three lakes. This lake sprawls across open terrain, providing views of the peaks on the south side of the old Donner Pass Road. The pristine nature of the area is compromised by a massive power line running along the west and north sides of the lake and a dam across the south end.

The next stage of your loop trip begins at the northwest tip of Lake Angela, from where a gully rises northwest up the hillside. Proceed up this gully, climbing on a moderate grade through light forest toward the crest of Boreal Ridge. Reach the top directly west of the easternmost high point, labeled 7665 on the *Norden* topo map. From the ridge you have splendid views of the Donner Pass region.

From the top of Boreal Ridge, descend into heavier forest on the north-facing hillside. Intersect your trail from the Sno-Park approximately 0.75 mile from the top of the ridge and follow your steps back to the car.

FYI: By leaving a car at Alpine Skills International at Donner Pass (see Trip 7 for directions), you can arrange a one-way, 2.5-mile shuttle trip between the Sno-Park on I-80 and the ASI parking lot on the old Donner Pass Road. However, this plan would eliminate the return trip over Boreal Ridge.

Warm-ups: Down in Truckee, El Toro Bravo will take the chill out of a cold winter's day with a wide selection of spicy Mexican dishes for lunch or dinner. Along with the traditional fare, the restaurant offers fajitas and seafood specialties like Capitola snapper and grilled Aptos prawns. Once the spicy food raises your temperature again, you can refresh yourself with a glass of sangria or an icy margarita. El Toro Bravo is on Donner Pass Road at the west end of Truckee's historic district. Call (530) 587-3557 for more information.

T R I P 9

Peter Grubb Hut & Round Valley

see map
on page
65

Duration: Full day
Distance: 5.25 miles round trip
Difficulty: Easy
Elevation: 7200/7900
Map: *Norden* 7.5′ quadrangle

Introduction: The easy access and short distance to Peter Grubb Hut make this trip extremely popular with skiers and snowshoers alike. Chances are, due to the popularity of this trip, you will be able to follow a packed trail all the way into Round Valley. Staying overnight at the hut provides a comfortable way to explore some of the backcountry to the north, insuring a degree of solitude, which will almost certainly be lacking on the trip to the hut. On clear days you have excellent views of Castle Peak and the Donner Summit area from Castle Pass.

How to get there: Just west of Donner Summit take the Castle Peak exit from Interstate 80. Follow signs to the Sno-Park at the east end of the frontage road immediately south of the freeway. To reach the trailhead you must walk back under the freeway to the north side of the westbound off-ramp.

Description: After walking under the freeway to the westbound off-ramp, begin your hike by following a snow-covered road that climbs above the ramp. Quickly the road turns northwest into mixed forest, where a pair of signs directs snowmobiles to the left and self-powered travelers to the right. Soon the route along the road leads to the open meadow of Castle Valley. Excellent views of the west face of Castle Peak appear as you pass slightly above and west of the valley bottom on a mild grade. Unless your trip happens to occur in the middle of a snowstorm, you should be able to follow the tracks of previous snowshoe or ski parties, due to the high popularity of this trip. Otherwise, periodically placed blue markers will help guide you.

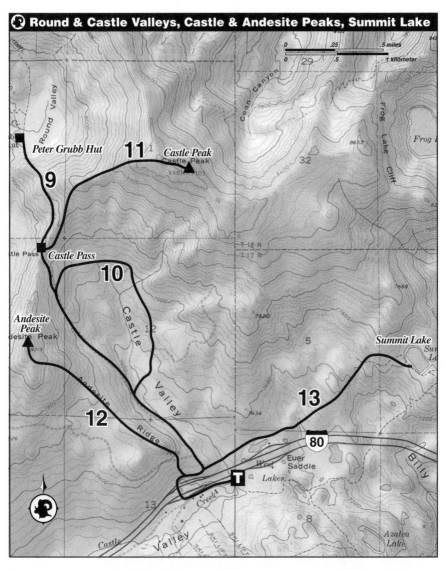

Leaving the meadow behind, you continue to ascend mildly up the valley through light-to-moderate forest cover. Near the head of the canyon the grade increases. At 2.25 miles from the trailhead you stand on top of Castle Pass, where an excellent vista appears of the peaks and ski areas of the Donner Summit region. The ramparts of Castle Peak loom directly above, while the ski runs of Northstar, Boreal Ridge, and Sugar Bowl are clearly seen carpeting the nearby hills.

Avoid the tendency to immediately descend from the pass, which leads to the snowmobile area. Instead, continue along the ridge northeast toward Castle Peak, following some old orange triangular signs marked SIERRA SKI WAY, CASTLE PEAK NORDEN. Eventually the route leaves the ridge and makes a mild descent through light forest for 0.5 mile to the edge of the hill overlooking beautiful Round Valley. Now descend more steeply to the edge of the valley and work your way over to Peter Grubb Hut.

The hut is a pleasant destination for a half-day outing, or a fine base camp for further explorations into the lonely territory to the north. The gentle, open slopes of Round Valley provide the perfect environment for skiers practicing their kick-and-glide technique.

Retrace your steps back to the trailhead.

FYI: To spend a night or two at the hut, contact the Sierra Club for reservations at:

Clair Tappaan Lodge
P.O. Box 36
Norden, CA 95724
(530) 426-3632

Warm-ups: The Cottonwood, high on the hill south of Truckee near the base of what was once California's first ski jump, is a consensus winner for one

Peter Grubb Hut

of North Tahoe's top restaurants. You would never guess from the ramshackle appearance of the building's exterior that the inside of the establishment is warm and inviting. The slightly eclectic menu changes daily, but usually offers a number of intriguing delights. While one of Truckee's oldest and best restaurants, the Cottonwood is also one of the most expensive as well. The Cottonwood is just off Brockway Road at 10142 Rue Hilltop. Call (530) 587-5711 for reservations or more information. You can salivate over their menu and sample excerpts from several reviews at **www.cottonwoodrestaurant.com.**

TRIP 10

Castle Valley Loop

Duration: One-half day
Distance: 3.75 miles partial loop trip
Difficulty: Easy
Elevation: 7200/7795
Map: *Norden* 7.5′ quadrangle

see map
on page
65

Introduction: By virtue of the 7227-foot elevation and the fairly dependable access of Interstate 80, Donner Summit provides snowshoers and skiers alike with access to some of the best conditions in the Sierra. Fair-weather winter weekends will see plenty of adventurous souls cavorting across the slopes of Boreal Ridge or propelling themselves into the backcountry on the opposite side of the highway. Fortunately, enough options exist to disperse these hearty recreationists across the snow-covered slopes of the Donner Summit region (see Trips 7–13).

Perhaps one of the easiest routes to be enjoyed in this area is the relatively simple jaunt around Castle Valley. Requiring only mild climbing and reasonably straightforward routefinding, combined with a short length, this trip is well suited to snowshoers of all levels. Blue diamonds will aid in finding the way through the forested sections, but the configuration of Castle Valley should present few navigational problems. In addition, even though most of the route passes through timber, the meadow at the lower end of Castle Valley provides a nice view of dramatically rugged Castle Peak.

How to get there: Just west of Donner Summit take the Castle Peak exit from Interstate 80. Follow signs to the Sno-Park at the east end of the frontage road immediately south of the freeway. To reach the trailhead you must walk back under the freeway to the north side of the westbound off-ramp.

Description: After walking under the freeway to the westbound off-ramp, begin your hike by following a snow-covered road that climbs above the ramp. Quickly the road turns northwest into mixed forest, where a pair of signs directs snowmobiles to the left and self-powered travelers to the right. Soon the route along the road leads to the open meadow of Castle Valley. Excellent views of the west face of Castle Peak appear as you pass slightly above and west of the valley bottom on a mild grade. Unless your trip happens to occur in the middle of a snowstorm, you should be able to follow the tracks of previous snowshoe or ski parties, due to the high popularity of this trip. Otherwise, periodically placed blue markers will help guide you.

Leaving the meadow behind, you continue to ascend mildly up the valley through light-to-moderate forest cover to where the grade of the slope increases below Castle Pass.

From just below the pass make a slightly descending traverse to the east through the trees to the far side of the drainage of Castle Valley. Continue the descent as the route bends to the south following the east edge of the valley through the forest. At 2.75 miles you break out into open meadows and traverse the clearing for a half mile until you rejoin the road, thereby closing the loop.

After meeting the road you should retrace your steps for another 0.75 mile back to the Sno-Park.

FYI: Individuals or groups interested in a guided tour in the Castle Peak or other Tahoe National Forest areas can contact Snowshoe Tours with Cathy-Works at (530) 273-6876, by email at cathyworks@oro.net, or by regular mail at 17639 Cindy Lane, Grass Valley, CA 95945. In addition to the guide service, snowshoes, lessons, and permits are included in the reasonable fee.

Warm-ups: Wong's Garden is the place in Truckee for Szechuan cuisine. Located at 11430 Deerfield Drive, Wong's is open for lunch at 11 A.M. and closes after dinner around 9 P.M. Call (530) 587-1831 for more information.

TRIP **11**

Castle Peak

see map
on page
65

Duration: Full day
Distance: 6.25 miles round trip
Difficulty: Difficult
Elevation: 7200/9103
Map: *Norden* 7.5' quadrangle

Introduction: The rugged ramparts of Castle Peak are a dominant feature of the Donner Summit landscape. At 9103 feet, the peak towers above the surrounding countryside, dwarfing the nearby hills and ridges. Coveted by alpinists and ski-mountaineers alike, the climb to the top provides a stimulating challenge for those up to the task. The first 2.25 miles to Castle Pass as described in Trip 9 are relatively mild, gaining only 725 vertical feet. However, the climb from the pass to the summit is an entirely different story, gaining 1200 feet in a mere one mile. Only those comfortable with high-angle slopes should consider climbing above the pass. Once atop the peak the effort is well rewarded by stunning views of the north Lake Tahoe countryside.

How to get there: Just west of Donner Summit take the Castle Peak exit from Interstate 80. Follow signs to the Sno-Park at the east end of the frontage road immediately south of the freeway. To reach the trailhead you must walk back under the freeway to the north side of the westbound off-ramp.

Description: After walking under the freeway to the westbound off-ramp, begin your hike by following a snow-covered road that climbs above the ramp. Quickly the road turns northwest into mixed forest, where a pair of signs directs snowmobiles to the left and self-powered travelers to the right. Soon the route along the road leads to the open meadow of Castle Valley. Excellent views of the west face of Castle Peak appear as you pass slightly above and west of the valley bottom on a mild grade. Unless your trip happens to occur in the middle of a snowstorm, you should be able to follow the tracks of previous snowshoe or ski parties, due to the high popularity of this trip. Otherwise, periodically placed blue markers will help guide you.

Leaving the meadow behind, you continue to ascend mildly up the valley through light-to-moderate forest cover. Near the head of the canyon the grade increases. At 2.25 miles from the trailhead you stand on top of Castle Pass, where an excellent vista appears of the peaks and ski areas of the Donner Summit region. The ramparts of Castle Peak loom directly above, while the ski runs of Northstar, Boreal Ridge, and Sugar Bowl are clearly seen carpeting the nearby hills.

From the 7930-foot pass head moderately steeply up the west ridge of Castle Peak. Higher up the ridge, bear slightly north of the ridge line and follow the less precipitous slopes toward the summit. Nearing the top, turn southeast to the true summit at 9103 feet. Depending on the conditions, some parties may feel more comfortable ascending the final pitch sans snowshoes. From the top of Castle Peak you have extraordinary views of the Donner Summit region as well as north to Sierra Buttes and south to the peaks of Desolation Wilderness.

When you have had your fill of the spectacular scenery, retrace your steps to the trailhead.

FYI: If you prefer not to retrace your steps, with a little navigation, you can descend the southeast ridge of Castle Peak and loop back to the trailhead.

Warm-ups: The Passage is another favorite Truckee dining establishment, located inside the historic 4-story Truckee Hotel. Restored to Victorian splendor over a decade ago, the hotel, restaurant, and bar are popular with tourists and locals alike. The Passage serves excellent food for lunch (Monday–Friday), brunch on the weekend, and dinner nightly. The award-winning wine list is highly touted. Find the Truckee Hotel across from the train station at the intersection of Bridge Street and Commercial Row. Call (530) 587-7619 for reservations or more information.

Castle Peak

TRIP **12**

Andesite Peak

see map
on page
65

Duration: One-half day
Distance: 3.5 miles round trip
Difficulty: Moderate
Elevation: 7200/8219
Map: *Norden* 7.5' quadrangle

Introduction: The ascent to Andesite Peak is a reasonably short hike to fantastic views of the northern realm of the Lake Tahoe region. The vistas are nearly as good as those from the summit of Castle Peak, which requires an additional 3 miles and 900 vertical feet to reach. Except for a couple of steep slopes, one near the beginning and one at the end, the trip would be classified as easy, since the navigation is fairly straightforward—gain the ridge and follow it to the top. A lack of popularity will almost guarantee an uncrowded journey. Certainly you should see fewer people than on the Castle Peak route.

Trailhead: Just west of Donner Summit take the Castle Peak exit from Interstate 80. Follow signs to the Sno-Park at the east end of the frontage road immediately south of the freeway. To reach the trailhead you must walk back under the freeway to the north side of the westbound off-ramp.

Description: After walking under the freeway to the westbound off-ramp, begin your hike by following a snow-covered road that climbs above the ramp. Immediately leave the road and head directly up the tree-covered slope below Andesite Ridge. After 0.1 mile, you will intersect a road heading west. Follow it a short distance, until you find a convenient place from which to begin a curving ascent of the steep slopes below Point 7605 shown on the *Norden* topo map. The immediate goal is to reach the top of Andesite Ridge just below and northwest of Point 7605.

Once the ridge is gained, the grade eases considerably as you stride northwest along Andesite Ridge. The scattered forest allows for sublime views of Castle Peak and the Donner Summit area. Straight ahead lies your goal, Andesite Peak. The next half mile provides easy snowshoeing across mild terrain, eventually returning to moderate forest cover below the base of the peak. Avoid the extreme east edge of Andesite Ridge and Andesite Peak, as large cornices may be present.

The grade increases dramatically as you approach the last 600 vertical feet to the summit. Initially the route passes through more heavy timber, but your perseverance will be rewarded higher up the slopes as the trees begin to thin again where you have dramatic views of Castle Peak. Continue to ascend until the terrain begins to ease just below the final ridge leading to the broad summit of Andesite Peak.

The 360° view from the summit is quite spectacular. Castle Peak looms majestically to the northeast, while off in the distance in all directions you have an incredible panorama of the peaks of north Tahoe.

Retrace your steps to the trailhead.

FYI: Varying your return to the Sno-Park is possible by descending north to Castle Pass, then reversing the description in Trip 9.

Warm-ups: Individuals or groups interested in a guided tour in the Castle Peak vicinity or other areas of the Tahoe National Forest can contact Cathy-Works by phone at (530) 273-6876, by email at info@cathyworks.com, or by regular mail at 17639 Cindy Lane, Grass Valley, CA 95945. Additional information is available on the website at **www.cathyworks.com**. In addition to the guide service, snowshoes, lessons, and permits are included in the reasonable fee.

On top of Andesite Peak

TRIP **13**

Summit Lake

see map
on page
65

Duration: One-half day
Distance: 4.25 miles round trip
Difficulty: Moderate
Elevation: 7200/7475
Map: *Norden* 7.5' quadrangle

Introduction: The trip to Summit Lake provides a pleasant alternative to the "freeway" leading to Peter Grubb Hut. However, without a marked trail or road to follow, you will have to put your routefinding skills to the test. The open terrain along the way provides some spectacular scenery of the Donner Summit region, and the secluded lake is a worthy destination for snowshoers looking for a peaceful half-day trip away from the crowds.

How to get there: Just west of Donner Summit take the Castle Peak exit from Interstate 80. Follow signs to the Sno-Park at the east end of the frontage road immediately south of the freeway. To reach the trailhead you must walk back under the freeway to the north side of the westbound off-ramp.

Description: After walking under the freeway to the westbound off-ramp, begin your hike by following a snow-covered road that climbs above the ramp. Proceed along the road until it quickly bends northwest. At this point leave the road and head east-northeast, roughly parallel to Interstate 80. Cross the ravine that drains Castle Valley and work your way over to the slope just above the westbound highway rest area.

From above the rest area, begin to head northeast slightly away from the highway. Although the trip in general does not gain a great deal of elevation, the topography is such that you must work your way over to hummocks, across drainages, and around minor hills, continually negotiating minor elevation changes. Try to maintain a direct route by following a visual fix on a point at the end of the southeast ridge extending down from Castle Peak. Summit Lake nestles in a shallow basin just below the end of that ridge.

Unless the day is so windy that you need the protection of the trees, you can set a course through open terrain for most of your route to the lake. Out in the open you have excellent views of the Castle Peak and Donner Summit areas, providing plenty of landmarks to help keep you on track, such as Interstate 80 and Boreal Ridge Ski Area. As you make the final approach, the best route stays well above the level of the lake, avoiding some steep terrain to the south that plunges down toward the highway. Cross the crest of a minor ridge and drop down to the lake, which is surrounded by a moderate forest of pine and fir. Summit Lake, pristine in appearance, provides only relative tranquility as the din from traffic on Interstate 80 is not completely out of earshot.

FYI: Parking at the westbound rest area of Interstate 80 and beginning your trip from there would save nearly a mile of additional snowshoeing over starting from the Donner Summit Sno-Park. Unfortunately, parking there for recreational purposes is illegal and thereby subject to fine.

Warm-ups: One of the old standbys in Truckee is O.B.'s Pub and Restaurant. The rustic décor accented with antiques hints at the thirty-plus years that O.B.'s has been serving locals and tourists alike. Located across from the fire station in the heart of Truckee's historic district, O.B.'s serves lunch and dinner daily and brunch on Sundays. Call (530) 587-4164 to make a reservation, or view a menu on their website at **www.obstruckee.com**.

Above Summit Lake

TRIP **14**

Donner Memorial State Park Loop

Duration: One-half day
Distance: 2.5 miles loop trip
Difficulty: Easy
Elevation: 5935/5975
Maps: *Truckee & Norden* 7.5′ quadrangles

see map on page 76

Introduction: The essentially flat landscape of Donner Memorial State Park is a great place for neophytes in need of some easy terrain where they can become accustomed to walking on snowshoes. The gentle topography provides a safe and easy environment for families with children as well. Even for the more advanced snowshoer, the park loop is a fine place to spend a morning or afternoon wandering through the scattered trees and catching glimpses of the lake. Incorporating a visit to the Emigrant Trail Museum along with a meal at one of the many fine establishments of Truckee makes for an excellent outing.

How to get there: From Interstate 80, take the exit for Donner Memorial State Park near the west end of Truckee and follow signs to the Sno-Park.

Description: The Nordic Trail begins at the west end of the Sno-Park. Follow the snow-covered road across the bridge over Donner Creek, avoiding the set cross-country ski tracks, and then move quickly to the marked junction with your return route on a road to the south. From this junction, continue west along the road as it follows the curving shoreline of Donner Lake. After a mile you bend around China Cove and then follow the marked route as it heads east for nearly one more mile. You then bend north for 0.25 mile and reach the junction mentioned previously that closes the loop. From there retrace your steps the short distance to the parking area.

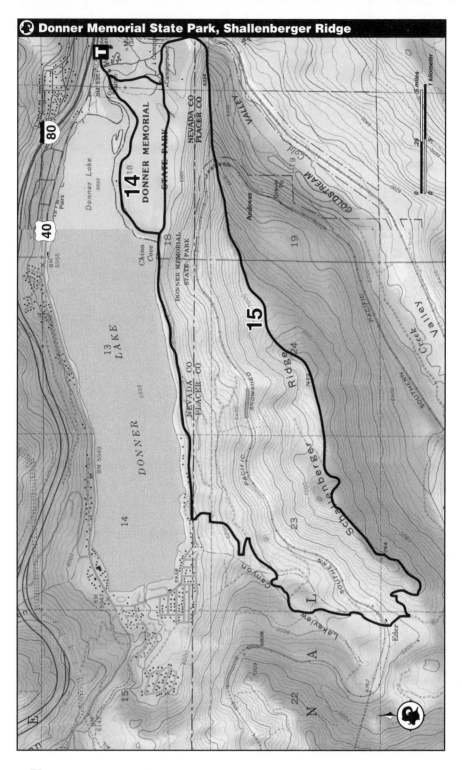

FYI: The Emigrant Trail Museum, dedicated in part to the fateful Donner Party mishap, is open from 9 A.M. to 4 P.M. There is a $2 fee for adults and $1 for children (6–12). Sno-Park permits can be purchased at the museum. For more information, call (530) 582-7892.

Warm-ups: The Donner Lake Kitchen, on Donner Pass Road near the north shore of the lake, is a favorite breakfast hangout of both locals and out-of-towners on weekends. The rustic cafe serves hearty portions sure to keep your engine stoked while on the trail. Some years the cafe closes for a week during the winter. Otherwise you can sink your teeth into their delectable fare seven days a week, from 7 A.M. to 2 P.M. (530) 587-3119.

TRIP **15**

Donner Lake– Schallenberger Ridge Loop

see map on page 76

Duration: Full day
Distance: 9.75 miles loop trip
Difficulty: Difficult
Elevation: 5935/7469
Maps: *Truckee & Norden* 7.5' quadrangles

Introduction: Modern-day visitors, armed with good equipment, fairly reliable weather forecasts, and accurate maps, now flock to an area that was once the site of perhaps the best-known tragedy of the westward expansion. Surprised by November snows, members of the Donner Party holed up at Donner Lake in an ill-fated attempt to survive the harsh conditions of the winter of 1846–47. Out of the 87 who began the trip in Illinois, only 47 were eventually rescued and led to safety over Donner Pass and down to the more hospitable climate in the valleys of California.

A century and a half later, snowshoers can experience the beauty of a winter wonderland that was no doubt lost on these unfortunate pioneers. Donner Lake is beautiful in its own right, but travelers along Schallenberger Ridge enjoy the added treat of stunning views of some of the Tahoe Sierra's most notable landmarks. A mere 2 miles east of Donner Pass, numerous peaks can be seen, including Mt. Lincoln, Anderson Peak, and Castle Peak. While visitors confront the bustling human activity in the town of Truckee and the whizzing traffic along the concrete ribbon of Interstate 80, snowshoers may feel as though they are in a different world altogether as they travel along the remote crest route.

This trip, like the grisly tale of the Donner Party, is not for the faint of heart. Completing the full journey requires the better part of a day, especially if snowshoers must plod through untracked powder. Although the route is generally straightforward, some routefinding is necessary, especially when searching for the most direct route down Lakeview Canyon. One potential drawback for some may be the one-mile walk along the plowed section of road through the housing area on the south shore of Donner Lake between Lakeview Canyon and Donner Lake Park.

How to get there: From Interstate 80, take the exit for Donner Memorial State Park near the west end of Truckee and follow signs to the Sno-Park.

Description: From the Sno-Park, follow the Donner Park Nordic Trail across the bridge over Donner Creek and then quickly to a trail junction. Turn south and proceed along the marked route for approximately one-third mile to where the Nordic Loop Trail bends west. Leave the Nordic Trail at this point and work your way east and then south around a pond to the snow-covered road leading into Coldstream Valley. Once upon the road, climb a short distance to where the road crosses the eastern extension of Schallenberger Ridge, near 1 mile from the trailhead.

Leaving the road here, climb moderately steeply up the nose of the hill through a light forest of fir and pine. After the initial climb the terrain eases somewhat as you begin to have views through a more scattered forest down into Coldstream Valley and up the canyon toward the ridge between Anderson Peak and Mt. Lincoln. Along the way toward the high point at 7469 feet, you climb through sections of open ridge crest and light forest. Once you reach the apex of Schallenberger Ridge, 3 miles from the Sno-Park, views expand to include Donner Peak and Mt. Judah to the west, Boreal Ridge and Castle Peak to the northwest, Mt. Rose and the Carson Range to the east, and a host of other landmarks including Donner Lake, Interstate 80, and Donner Pass Road.

Now you descend along the ridge through light-to-scattered forest to a saddle and then make a short, moderate climb up the hill 0.75-mile west of Peak 7469.

Nearly level walking along the ridge brings you to better views where the trees thin again. Soon the ridge narrows and you make a brief descent into the next saddle before a short climb leads up to Peak 7264.

From Peak 7264, you follow the narrow crest of Schallenberger Ridge on a moderate descent toward the broad, forested saddle above Lakeview Canyon. At the saddle you encounter a road, 4.75 miles from the Sno-Park. Unless you are here during or immediately after a storm, there should be plenty of tracks on this route as snowmobilers use this road as a connection between Donner Lake and Coldstream Valley.

You turn north and follow the road on a winding descent for 0.25 mile. As you approach the railroad tracks, the road bends west, paralleling the tracks for 0.5 mile before crossing over and continuing down Lakeview Canyon. Rather than follow the road, carefully head straight across the tracks near Eder, an abandoned railroad stop as shown on the *Norden* topo map. Once safely across you must negotiate the short, steep slope on the downhill side of the tracks.

Beyond the tracks, make your way north across the gentle terrain to the west branch of the seasonal creek that drains Lakeview Canyon. Find the continuation of the road nearby and follow its winding course down through the canyon to the paved road above the south shore of Donner Lake, 7 miles from your starting point.

For the next mile you will be forced to abandon your snowshoes and walk the plowed road past the homes along the south side of the lake, as the road is kept open for residents during the winter. Once you reach the end of

View from Shallenberger Ridge

the plowed section, you can don your snowshoes again and proceed on a gentle downhill grade, crossing the western boundary of Donner State Park near China Cove, 8.5 miles from the trailhead.

You proceed through the park for a short distance until reaching a groomed turnaround. Veer north at this point and then follow the north branch of the Nordic loop trail around China Cove and east along the south shore of Donner Lake. Just beyond the end of the lake you encounter a Y-junction, from which you should continue straight for another 250 yards to a T-junction. Closing the loop here, you turn left, following an exit sign, cross the bridge over Donner Creek, and quickly conclude your journey at the parking lot.

FYI: Avoid the north edge of Schallenberger Ridge, where nasty cornices may develop.

Warm-ups: Pianeta Ristorante at 10096 Donner Pass Road in the historic section of Truckee offers traditional Italian fare with a Tahoe twist. The food may be sublime and the frescoed interior classic, but Gore-Tex and pile-clad recreationists will feel right at home in the casual atmosphere. The restaurant has a full bar and a decent wine list featuring a sampling of Italian wines. Reservations are recommended on weekends (530) 587-4694.

Sign along trail, Donner State Park

T R I P **16**

Brockway Summit to Peak 7766

see map
on page
82

Duration: One-half day
Distance: 1.25 miles round trip
Difficulty: Moderate
Elevation: 7125/7766
Map: *Martis Peak* 7.5' quadrangle

Introduction: A short but steep ascent leads to a supreme view of Lake Tahoe and the encircling mountains. In the summer, hikers can follow the newly built Tahoe Rim Trail nearly a mile to a junction with a spur trail up to this wonderful vista. However, snowfall has a way of obliterating well-defined summer trails, and this particular route is no exception. Attempting to successfully follow this trail in winter can be daunting, so this description below forsakes the standard route and climbs directly up the hillside to the top of Peak 7766.

Although the climb begins in dense timber, the route is simple—climb up the slope until you can't climb any higher. Near the top the forest barrier eases, climaxing in a nearly treeless vista from the top of the peak. The view of Lake Tahoe and neighboring peaks is a truly great reward for the relatively brief effort.

How to get there: Follow State Highway 267, southbound from Truckee or northbound from Kings Beach, to the plowed shoulder just 0.5 mile southeast of Brockway Summit. Depending on the snow depth, you may find hiker emblems or Tahoe Rim Trail signs alongside the highway.

Description: Cross the highway to the northeast shoulder and begin snowshoeing up Forest Road 56 to the summer trailhead for this section of the Tahoe Rim Trail. The TRT bends west from the trailhead, but the snow-covered trail is difficult to discern beyond the beginning of a series of switchbacks that zigzag up the moderately forested hillside. Therefore, if you

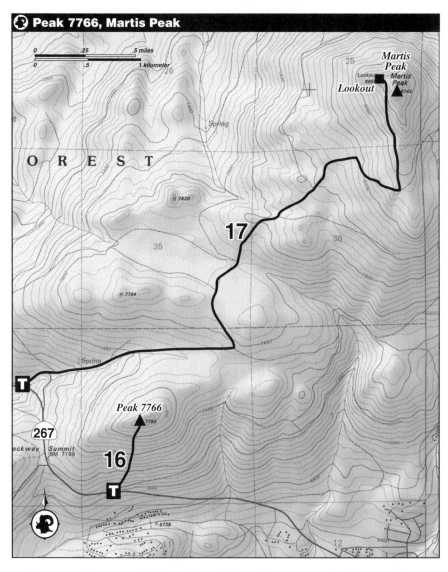

don't mind the steep climb, perhaps the simplest way up the slope is a direct climb toward the ridge crest above.

You climb up the hillside moderately steeply through thick ponderosa pines. Even though the timber doesn't allow you to gain your bearings on the initial part of the ascent, the routefinding is straightforward—head for the top. The higher you climb, the less dense the forest becomes, granting a small prelude to the upcoming view from the peak. Once you reach the sparsely forested, long summit ridge, stunning views of Lake Tahoe and the surrounding countryside are a fine reward. A clear day promises exquisite views of one of California's most prominent natural treasures. Lake Tahoe shimmers in the midwinter sun, surrounded by Sierra peaks on all sides. To the west, Silver Peak presides over the northwest shore. Mt. Tallac dominates the southwest side of the lake, backed by the rugged peaks of Desolation Wilderness. The triangular summit of Freel Peak rises above the southeast shore as the Tahoe Basin's highest summit at 10,881 feet, while the ski runs of Heavenly Valley lie in Freel's shadow. The highest mountain seen on the east side of the lake is Snow Valley Peak. Nearby is Martis Peak, where careful observation reveals the lookout nestled on a ridge immediately northwest of the true summit. Just beyond Martis Peak to the southeast is Mt. Baldy, lying just within the Mt. Rose Wilderness boundary.

FYI: Snowboarders may want to pack along their gear for the thrilling descent. However, caution should be exercised on the lower part of the run through the dense timber.

Warm-ups: The Log Cabin Café in Kings Beach has been voted more than once as the best place for breakfast in North Tahoe. Located on the main drag at 8692 North Lake Blvd, the small café serves up ample portions of standard breakfast fare, as well as a number of unique dishes. Try the Cajun Eggs Benedict, a spicy twist on the traditional dish that is the house specialty and has been featured in *Bon Appetit* magazine. Open seven days a week, the popular restaurant is very busy on weekends. (530) 546-7109

The Squeeze Inn offers breakfast aficionados a bounty of unusually named omelettes that will surely satisfy the tastebuds of the most finicky diner. Each omelette comes with a choice of three sauces along with yummy potatoes and whole wheat toast. A small selection of traditional fare is offered for anti-omelette eaters. The rustic cafe is located in the heart of the historic district of Truckee and is open from 7 A.M. to 2 P.M. (530) 587-9814.

TRIP **17**

Martis Peak

Duration: Three-quarter day
Distance: 8 miles round trip
Difficulty: Moderate
Elevation: 7000/8742
Map: *Martis Peak* 7.5′ quadrangle

see map on page 82

Introduction: Martis Peak is a popular trip for skiers and snowshoers alike, and with good reason. The 4-mile climb to the summit is relatively easy, thanks to a predominantly mild grade and a readily discernible Forest Service road that is periodically marked by blue diamonds. Most likely, thanks to the popularity of the route, you won't have to break trail, unless you're the first one there after a fresh snowfall. The forested road leads to a restored fire lookout, at one time the only manned outpost in the Tahoe Basin, from where you have incomparable views of Lake Tahoe.

How to get there: Reach Highway 267 from Interstate 80 in Truckee, or from Lake Tahoe off Highway 28 in Kings Beach. Travel south from I-80 or north from Hwy. 28 on Hwy. 267 to Martis Peak Road, 0.4 mile north of Brockway Summit (9 miles from I-80 and 3.5 from Hwy. 28). Park in the small plowed area on the east side of the highway at the beginning of Martis Peak Road. Parking is limited, especially on weekends, so leave as much room as possible for other vehicles.

Description: Begin your trip by climbing east up the road on a moderate grade through a mixed forest of white fir and ponderosa and lodgepole pine. The grade eases after the first 0.75 mile as you ascend mildly through medium forest cover. Even if tracks have not been set by previous skiers or snowshoers, the alignment of the road is obvious. After proceeding straight ahead for 1.3 miles, you reach a junction and turn sharply left (north), following a brown Forest Service ski marker.

Continue to climb up the road, the mild climb briefly interrupted by a couple of short descents. Pass through a small clearing, over a flat knoll, across another small clearing and back into the forest, where you come to another junction. Follow the road to the right around a sweeping turn and begin a more moderate climb, angling up the hillside. Where the moderate ascent levels, 3.25 miles from the highway, turn 90 degrees left onto a road leading north to the lookout on Martis Peak.

As you make the moderate climb up the road, the forest begins to thin, allowing for some limited views of the surrounding countryside. The grade increases over the last 0.25 mile until you reach the saddle and the Martis Peak fire lookout, 4 miles from Highway 267.

The lookout has been restored, thanks to a joint effort involving the California Department of Forestry and the U.S. Forest Service. Improvements to the wooden building include double-paned windows and a linoleum floor. Feel free to use the lookout, but with proper respect for the historical landmark and the hard work necessary for its restoration. Although previous parties have camped in the lookout, you should obey the ban on fires and cooking if staying overnight. The structure provides a wonderful setting for enjoying the supreme view of Lake Tahoe and the neighboring forest land. Near the lookout you may find a picnic table and an outhouse on the windblown ridge.

If you wish to reach the actual summit of Martis Peak, you must follow the ridge southeast another 0.1 mile and 86 vertical feet from the lookout to the top of the 8,742-foot mountain.

Martis Peak Lookout

FYI: Taking a pair of cross-country skis for the descent permits a thrilling ride from the summit all the way back to the car.

Warm-ups: The Squeeze Inn offers breakfast aficionados a bounty of unusually named omelettes that will surely satisfy the tastebuds of the most finicky diner. Each omelette comes with a choice of three sauces along with yummy potatoes and whole wheat toast. A small selection of traditional fare is offered for anti-omelette eaters. The rustic cafe is located in the heart of the historic district of Truckee and is open from 7 A.M. to 2 P.M. (530) 587-9814.

The Log Cabin Café in Kings Beach has been voted more than once as the best place for breakfast in North Tahoe. Located on the main drag at 8692 North Lake Blvd, the small café serves up ample portions of standard breakfast fare, as well as a number of unique dishes. Try the Cajun Eggs Benedict, a spicy twist on the traditional dish that is the house specialty and has been featured in *Bon Appétit* magazine. Open seven days a week, the popular restaurant is very busy on weekends. (530) 546-7109

TRIP 18

Galena Creek

Duration: Three-quarter day (lower route)
or full day (upper route)
Distance: 4.25 miles shuttle trip via lower route
8 miles shuttle trip via upper route
Difficulty: Moderate (lower route) or difficult (upper route)
Elevation: 6775/8640 (lower route), 6775/9400 (upper route)
Maps: *Washoe City & Mount Rose* 7.5' quadrangles

see maps on pages 87, 88

Introduction: This trip grants snowshoers two options for taking in the pleasant scenery along Galena Creek. The most difficult stretch of trail, common to both routes, occurs shortly after the beginning of the trip, where the route leaves Galena Creek County Park and enters Forest Service land. The creek slices through tangled vegetation at the bottom of a deep, forested canyon, an obstacle that is surmounted by climbing high above the stream along a

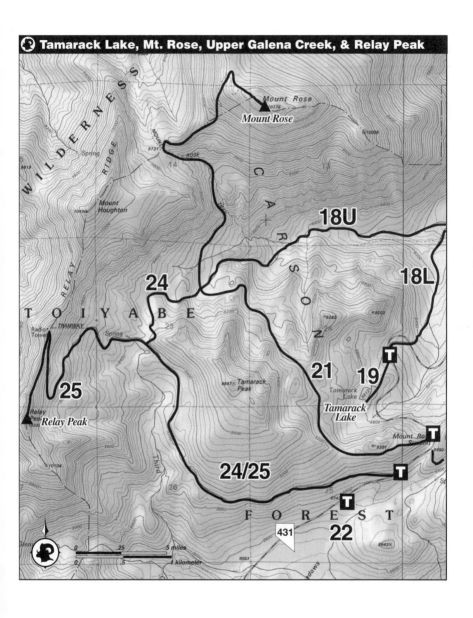

Tamarack Lake, Mt. Rose, Upper Galena Creek, & Relay Peak

steep hillside. Past there, the terrain eases and culminates in a broad, open canyon with picturesque views at the upper end.

Nearly twice as long as the lower route, the upper route passes through the best of the scenery in the upper canyon, eventually connecting with the Upper Galena Creek route described in Trip 24. The lower route certainly

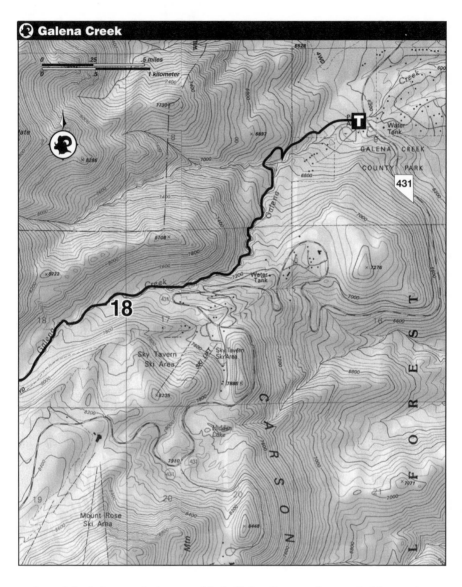

doesn't lack for good views and is half the distance, but probably requires slightly more sophisticated navigational skills.

How to get there: Travel on the Mt. Rose Highway (Nevada SR 431) to the south entrance of Galena Creek Park (7.25 miles west of the U.S. 395 freeway near Reno). There are two roads into Galena Creek Park, so be sure to turn into the well-marked south entrance. Park in the paved lot of the park.

LOWER ROUTE ENDING TRAILHEAD: Continue up the Mt. Rose Highway (Nevada SR 431) from the south entrance into Galena Creek Park 7.8 miles to the plowed parking area on the eastbound shoulder of the highway.

UPPER ROUTE ENDING TRAILHEAD: Head west on S.R. 431 to Mt. Rose Summit, at 8900 feet the highest winter-maintained road in the Sierra. From the summit descend 0.3 mile to the trailhead at the beginning of the access road near a concrete block building, where you may find limited parking for a handful of cars on the westbound shoulder. If parking spaces are unavailable, descend another 0.5 mile on the highway to the Tahoe Meadows trailhead, where you will find a plowed parking area on the eastbound shoulder. On busy winter weekends the parking lot fills quickly, and you might be forced to park on the shoulder of the busy highway.

If you are coming from Incline Village, the Tahoe Meadows trailhead is 7.75 miles east of the junction between the Mt. Rose Highway and State Route 28.

Description: Begin by crossing Galena Creek on a wooden bridge and then following the route of the Galena Creek Park nature trail up the north bank of the creek through a moderate forest of Jeffrey pine. Where the trail veers away from the creek, you must continue upstream, gaining the crest of the bank above. Approximately 0.5 mile from the parking lot, a tributary joins the main channel of Galena Creek. In order to surmount this obstacle you must head up the right-hand tributary a short distance and descend steeply to a crossing. Once across the tributary, work your way downstream slightly to a point where you can comfortably round the steep hillside separating the two branches and resume your climb up the main channel. Avoid the willow-choked streambed by climbing the steep hillside above the right-hand bank of the main channel of Galena Creek. The grade of the ascent eventually eases and makes for more pleasant snowshoeing, at least temporarily.

Soon the terrain grows steep again, and you are forced higher up the hillside above the creek. The goal in this section of the trip is to gain enough altitude to safely traverse the steep slopes of the canyon, which plunge directly into the creek bottom. Easier terrain appears 1.5 miles from the trailhead, as you approach the creek on gentler slopes. Some nice views of the south end of the Truckee Meadows and the Callahan Ranch area appear behind you.

As you climb up the creek, the Mt. Rose Highway appears across the drainage as well as the Sky Tavern Ski area, where the city of Reno runs the largest learn-to-ski program for elementary students in the nation. Solitude eventually returns as forward progress continues and the highway makes one of its many horseshoe bends on the way to the summit. You head along the creek over very pleasant terrain, passing around extensive stands of quaking aspen. Where Galena Creek makes a tight S-curve, a short rise briefly interrupts the agreeable ascent, above which the canyon opens up dramatically below the slopes of Mt. Rose. Just beyond the head of the canyon, you can see the microwave structures on top of Relay Ridge.

LOWER ROUTE ENDING TRAILHEAD: To reach the lower route-ending trailhead, you must cross Galena Creek 3 miles from the trailhead, near the confluence with the tributary branch of the creek that drains Tamarack Lake. After you find a convenient place to cross the main channel of Galena Creek, the other branch may not be particularly obvious as it will most likely be frozen and covered with snow. Look for the low spot in the ridge directly east of Peak 9202 and follow the subtle drainage south up moderate slopes through the trees until you reach a large meadow. Across the meadow you can see myriad skiers descending the multiple runs of the Mt. Rose Ski Area on Slide Mountain. From the meadow follow the course of the creek southeast into the trees and carefully across the Mt. Rose Highway up to the parking area.

UPPER ROUTE ENDING TRAILHEAD: Continue to ascend the gentle slopes next to the main branch of Galena Creek. The upper part of the canyon remains open terrain with picturesque views. For the next 2 miles the route follows the direct line of the creek as it cuts a course below the south flank of Mt. Rose. Approaching the head of the canyon, you eventually intersect the route of the Upper Galena Creek trip (Trip 24). Reverse the description in Trip 24, following the trail which soon leads to the access road. Follow the road for 2.5 more miles out to the Mt. Rose Highway.

FYI: This trip is best suited for times when there has been adequate snowfall at the lower elevations. Otherwise you may have to hike a considerable distance to reach satisfactory snow.

Warm-ups: Since the unfortunate closing of the Christmas Tree restaurant, recreationists traveling the Mt. Rose Highway will have to descend all the way to the western outskirts of Reno to find a decent eatery or watering hole. Snow-sodden snowshoers in search of plebian fare will enjoy Bully's Sports Bar and Grill in the Raley's shopping center at the northeast corner of the intersection of Mt. Rose Highway and Wedge Parkway. Voted best sports bar in northern Nevada every year since 1996, Bully's offers a wide variety of delectable dishes and satisfying beverages. You can check out their menu online at **www.bullyssportsbar.com**.

TRIP **19**

Tamarack Lake

see map on page 87

Duration: One-half day
Distance: 1 mile
Difficulty: Easy
Elevation: 8615/8835
Map: *Mount Rose* 7.5' quadrangle

Introduction: Snowshoers looking for a quick and relatively easy trip will find the journey to Tamarack Lake a good option, as the distance is short and the terrain is mostly mild except for a short, moderate stretch of climbing. Nestled beneath the shadow of Tamarack Peak, the lake and surrounding meadow are quite picturesque, with the combination of pleasant scenery and level terrain providing a fine destination for a morning or afternoon snowshoe.

How to get there: Follow the Mt. Rose Highway (State Route 431) to a plowed parking area on the eastbound shoulder of the road, 0.9 mile eastbound of Mt. Rose Summit.

Description: Carefully cross the highway and scale the snowbank on the uphill side. Head southwest away from the highway to the east of a tributary of Galena Creek draining Tamarack Lake. Make a brief ascent of a forested hillside to the apex of a mildly sloping ridge and follow it to the east side of snow-covered Tamarack Lake. From there, you can continue across the lake and the open meadow to the south before looping back around to the lake and retracing your steps to the parking area. If you have the extra time and energy, continuing up steeper terrain toward Tamarack Peak is a fine trip extension.

FYI: Since the slopes of Tamarack Peak are favored by snowboarders and backcountry skiers for the usually decent powder conditions and challenging terrain, snowshoers would be wise to either pack along some downhill gear and join them, or keep a watchful eye out in order to avoid an unnecessary encounter.

Snowshoers at Tamarack Lake

Warm-ups: Since the unfortunate closing of the Christmas Tree restaurant, winter recreationists traveling the Mt. Rose Highway must descend all the way toward the western outskirts of Reno to fine a decent eatery or watering hole. Those in search of a cocktail or an upscale dinner can stop at Sierra Solitaire Restaurant and Bar, 4 miles west of the U.S. 395 junction. Open Tuesday through Sunday, diners savor scrumptious entrees like wild salmon steak Vouvray, or lamb loin en croute chef Mordhorst. Call (775) 849-2100 for reservations. To view a menu, check out the website at **www.sierra-solitairerestaurant.com**.

Slide Mountain

see map
on page
94

Duration: One-half day
Distance: 2 miles round trip
Difficulty: Difficult
Elevation: 8900/9680
Map: *Mount Rose* 7.5′ quadrangle

Introduction: The view from the summit of Mt. Rose is highly prized, particularly in the summer when hundreds of weekend warriors struggle up the 5-mile trail. The number of successful summiteers who reach the top of Rose plummets dramatically in the winter, as a thick mantle of snow, frigid temperatures, and icy winds deter all but the most hardy recreationists from attempting the Tahoe Basin's third highest peak. Snowshoers who want a similar view with a fraction of the effort can accept the challenge of ascending neighboring Slide Mountain.

Although a much shorter trip than the journey to Rose, Slide is not without its own challenges. Just as snowy, chilly, and windy, Slide Mountain's topography forces snowshoers to make a steep ascent beyond the mild approach from the highway to the site of the Mt. Rose Campground near the western base of the peak. In addition, the last half of the route passes near the edge of the Mt. Rose Ski Area, which inhibits much chance of solitude for those seeking an opportunity to "get away from it all."

Those who reach the top will be greeted by extraordinary views to the west of Lake Tahoe and the surrounding mountains, and east of the Truckee Meadows and Washoe Valley backdropped by the peaks of the Virginia Range.

How to get there: Follow the Mt. Rose Highway, (State Route 431) to Mt. Rose Summit, which at 8900 feet is the highest winter-maintained road in the Sierra. Park your vehicle in the plowed area on the west side of the highway, which serves as the summer trailhead parking area for the Mt. Rose Trail.

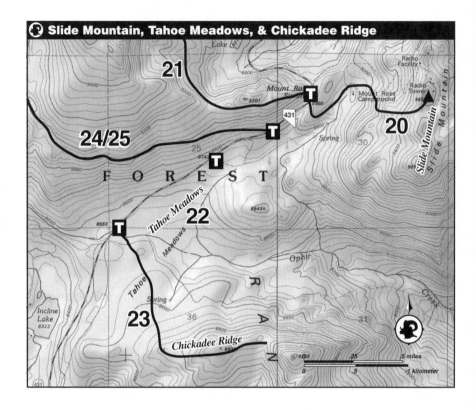

Slide Mountain, Tahoe Meadows, & Chickadee Ridge

Description: Carefully cross the highway to the east shoulder and begin snowshoeing on the snow-covered road that in the summer accesses the Mt. Rose Campground. Proceed along the road for about 0.4 mile to the site of the campground.

Leave the gently sloping terrain at the campground and begin a steep climb of the lightly forested slopes leading up toward the long summit ridge of Slide Mountain. Half way up the climb, you approach the boundary of the Mt. Rose Ski Area, which you should stay out of as long as the terrain allows. Farther up the slope you may have to cross the boundary to avoid some steep and difficult terrain. Nearing the top, you gain a minor ridge and veer toward the summit, which has a number of antennas, mechanical structures, and ski lift equipment littering the ridge. Views from the top are quite impressive of the Lake Tahoe basin to the west and basin and range topography to the east. Be prepared for very strong winds that typically blast the summit ridge.

FYI: Accomplished snowboarders and backcountry skiers may want to pack along their gear for a thrilling descent. However, those who plan on such a descent must stay out of the ski area boundary to avoid paying the price of a lift ticket.

Warm-ups: The Galena Market at the corner of Thomas Creek Road and Mt. Rose Highway on the southeastern outskirts of Reno has long been a supporter of outdoor pursuits. Snowshoes are available for rent at $10 per day plus refundable deposit. In addition to the usual convenience store items, the establishment has a small snack bar with booth and counter seating, serving a variety of breakfast items, cold sandwiches, and hot snacks, including pizza slices, chicken strips, and burritos. The café is open from 6:30 A.M. to 2 P.M. daily.

Snowshoer below Slide Mountain

Mt. Rose Summit

see map
on page
87

Duration: Full day
Distance: 10 miles round trip
Difficulty: Difficult
Elevation: 8900/10776
Map: *Mt. Rose* 7.5'quadrangle

Introduction: Hundreds of hikers may reach the summit of Mt. Rose on a busy summer weekend, but only a few daring souls accept the challenge of a winter ascent. Views from the third highest peak in the Tahoe basin are sublime, a worthwhile reward for the hearty effort. Most winter enthusiasts are content with a snowshoe to Upper Galena Creek (Trip 24) or Relay Peak (Trip 25) as their goal, but the challenge of ascending Mt. Rose appeals to more experienced snowshoers. The first half of the trip follows the route of a newly constructed section of the Mt. Rose Trail on an easy traverse and descent into Galena Creek basin. The second half is quite steep and subject to less than ideal snow conditions, as well as usually stiff winds above 9800 feet.

How to get there: Follow the Mt. Rose Highway, (State Route 431) to Mt. Rose Summit, which at 8900 feet is the highest winter-maintained road in the Sierra. Park your vehicle in the plowed area on the west side of the highway, which serves as the summer trailhead parking area for the Mt. Rose Trail.

Description: From the parking area, ascend a short but steep slope and then follow a rising traverse along a ridge above the Mt. Rose Highway, across mostly open slopes dotted with lodgepole and whitebark pines. Fine views of Tahoe Meadows and Lake Tahoe are plentiful from the ridge top before the route veers away from the highway toward a saddle between Peak 9201 on the right and Tamarack Peak on the left.

Beyond the saddle, you make a rising traverse across the eastern flank of Tamarack Peak, as mountain hemlocks join the pines. Mt. Rose can be seen over the tops of the trees at various points along the traverse. About 1.5

miles from the parking lot, you begin a mild descent across steep slopes on the northeast side of Tamarack Peak toward the floor of Galena Creek. At the bottom of your descent the route veers north across the basin and climbs moderately around the fringe of a meadow to the northern tributary of Galena Creek.

From the drainage, make a moderate ascent across an open hillside to a side canyon where you turn northwest up a much steeper grade. At the head of this canyon, you reach the crest of a ridge and turn northeast, heading along the ridge line. If the winds are howling, this is a good place to turn around and head back, as they will only get worse as you near the summit.

Follow the ridge for 0.5 mile until you encounter the summit massif of Mt. Rose, where the route begins to climb the northwest slope. After gaining 200 feet of elevation, make an ascending traverse toward the broad saddle separating Mt. Rose from Peak 10601. You'll probably encounter wind-packed snow conditions in this area, so carefully watch your footing. At the saddle, turn southeast and steeply ascend the final slopes to the summit.

The views from the top of Mt. Rose are quite impressive. On clear days following storms, you may be able to see all the way north to the Cascade volcanoes of Mt. Shasta and Lassen Peak. If the atmosphere is less kind, Sierra Buttes will be the prominent landmark on the northern horizon. To

Snowshoers with Mt. Rose in the background

the southwest, Mt. Tallac and Pyramid Peak stand guard over Desolation Wilderness and, to the south, the tri-peaks of Freel Peak, Jobs Peak, and Jobs Sister dominate the Carson Range. As one might expect, the crystalline waters of Lake Tahoe provide the centerpiece for the grandest of views from the summit.

If the winds are calm on top of Mt. Rose, consider yourself truly blessed. If not, your continued admiration of the views will probably be self-limiting as you urgently seek the less breezy conditions below. However long your stay, the short winter days will ultimately hasten your return as you retrace your steps to the trailhead.

FYI: As noted in the description, the winds on top of Mt. Rose can be severe. Even if the conditions at the trailhead appear benign, take along plenty of clothing for the potentially windy conditions on the 10,776-foot summit. The second half of the trip can be tedious, depending on the weather and snow conditions. Plan on an early start to avoid returning in the dark.

Warm-ups: Since the unfortunate closing of the Christmas Tree restaurant, winter recreationists traveling the Mt. Rose Highway must descend all the way toward the western outskirts of Reno to fine a decent eatery or watering hole. Those in search of a cocktail or an upscale dinner can stop at Sierra Solitaire Restaurant and Bar, 4 miles west of the U.S. 395 junction. Open Tuesday through Sunday, diners savor scrumptious entrees like wild salmon steak Vouvray, or lamb loin en croute chef Mordhorst. Call (775) 849-2100 for reservations. To view a menu, check out the website at **www.sierrasolitairerestaurant.com**.

TRIP **22**

Tahoe Meadows

see map
on page
94

Duration: One-half to three-quarter day
Distance: Varies
Difficulty: Easy to moderate
Elevation: 8550
Map: *Mount Rose* 7.5′ quadrangle

Introduction: Tahoe Meadows is a popular winter playground for residents of the Reno-Sparks area. A weekend of clear skies and fresh powder attracts hundreds of winter enthusiasts to the wide-open terrain and gentle slopes. In recent years the Forest Service has wisely banned snowmobiles entirely from the east side of the Mt. Rose Highway. Snowmobiling is now limited to the west side of the highway away from the well traveled meadows. Tahoe Meadows is heavily used by snowshoers, skiers, and sledders on weekends, but a high percentage of the crowd is reluctant to venture away from the heart of the meadows, and the throng all but disappears during the week. Snowshoers can leave the masses behind by venturing into the trees surrounding the meadows, or by heading down Ophir Creek toward Price Lake.

How to get there: The Tahoe Meadows trailhead is 0.4 mile westbound of the Mt. Rose Highway Summit. Parking may be limited on busy weekends, so arrive early to get a good spot. The Tahoe Meadows trailhead is 7.75 miles east of the junction of the Mt. Rose Highway and State Route 28 in Incline Village.

Description: The great thing about Tahoe Meadows is that you can tailor a trip to the skill level of your group and the time they have available. Loops around the meadows of varying lengths are quite easy to organize so that they will fit any group's agenda. Chilling winds do blow across the open meadows at times and when that is the case you should head for the edge of the meadows and the shelter of the forest.

A fine option for a longer trip is to head east across the meadows and continue down Ophir Creek canyon. The grade starts out fairly mild but increases the farther you travel downstream. Continuing all the way to Price Lake is possible, provided you remember that the 2.5-mile journey is all uphill on the way back.

FYI: Keep a careful eye on the weather. This is high country, and though it seems quite tame when the skies are clear, almost every year someone in this area is caught off guard by the deteriorating weather of a fast-moving Pacific storm. Over the years, poor decisions have resulted in a few deaths and numerous search-and-rescue operations.

Warm-ups: If you're headed back to Incline Village, stop by the Village Cafe and Roastery for fresh-roasted coffees, fresh-baked pastries, and homemade soups made from old family recipes. Located on Tahoe Blvd. between 7-11 and the Cinema, the Village Cafe closes at 5 P.M.

Snowshoer in Tahoe Meadows

T R I P **23**

Chickadee Ridge

see map on page **94**

Duration: One-half day
Distance: 3 miles round trip
Difficulty: Easy to moderate
Elevation: 8550/9225
Map: *Mount Rose* 7.5′ quadrangle

Introduction: Tahoe Meadows is a busy place, particularly on weekends. You can minimize the effect the hordes of snowshoers, cross-country skiers, and families involved in snow play create next to the highway by venturing away from the meadows on this trip that roughly follows a part of the route of the Tahoe Rim Trail. The trip begins in the meadows, passes through a lodgepole pine forest, and then climbs up to a wonderful view of Lake Tahoe from a ridge that locals refer to as Chickadee Ridge, after the black-headed birds that frequent the area. Most groups will be satisfied with the ridgecrest view as a turnaround point, but hardier snowshoers can continue up steeper slopes to the top of Peak 9225 for even better views of the lake and the surrounding peaks.

How to get there: The Tahoe Meadows trailhead is 0.4 mile westbound of the Mt. Rose Highway Summit. Parking may be limited on busy weekends, so arrive early to get a good spot. The Tahoe Meadows trailhead is 7.75 miles east of the junction of the Mt. Rose Highway and State Route 28 in Incline Village.

Description: From the south edge of the meadows, head southwest on a gentle grade through lodgepole-pine forest. Soon you begin climbing, mildly at first and then more moderately as you approach the lower slopes of Chickadee Ridge, where lighter forest allows you to take your bearings on the peak ahead. Approaching the top of Chickadee Ridge, you have partial views of Lake Tahoe through scattered whitebark pines, a portent of better things soon to come. Once you have gained the crest, Tahoe is revealed in all its glory. You traverse across the hillside on the west side of the ridge with nearly continuous lake views along the way. By gaining the crest, the views expand to include Tahoe Meadows below and Mt. Rose across the highway.

To reach Peak 9225 you must follow the ridge to the base of the peak. The final climb to the summit will prove to be too steep for skis, but with a pair of modern snowshoes you should be able to negotiate the last 200 feet. You may have to pick your way around exposed boulders on the wind-blown slopes, but the view from the peak is a worthy reward. From the summit of Peak 9225 the north part of Lake Tahoe lies at your feet. To the southwest, the peaks of Desolation Wilderness rise above forested terrain. Near at hand, all of Tahoe Meadows, as well as Mt. Rose and Slide Mountain, appear close enough to reach out and touch.

You can easily extend your journey by continuing south along the spine of the Carson Range. The mostly open terrain allows nearly continuous views alternating between the Lake Tahoe basin to the west and Washoe and Carson valleys to the east. Retrace your steps to the trailhead.

FYI: Your trip to Chickadee Ridge will almost certainly include several visits by the namesake birds, especially if you stop along the way for a snack. The birds have become quite tame, having been the recipients of numerous handouts from humans over the years. Pack along a zip-lock bag full of birdseed if you don't think you'll be able to resist the urge to feed them. Please don't use human food, particularly junk food like Twinkies or M&Ms.

Lake Tahoe from Chickadee Ridge

Warm-ups: The Galena Market at the corner of Thomas Creek Road and Mt. Rose Highway on the southeastern outskirts of Reno has long been a supporter of outdoor pursuits. Snowshoes are available for rent at $10 per day plus refundable deposit. In addition to the usual convenience store items, the establishment has a small snack bar with booth and counter seating, serving a variety of breakfast items, cold sandwiches, and hot snacks, including pizza slices, chicken strips, and burritos. The café is open from 6:30 A.M. to 2:00 P.M. daily.

TRIP 24

Upper Galena Creek

Duration: One-half day
Distance: 6 miles round trip
Difficulty: Easy
Elevation: 8835/9200
Map: *Mount Rose* 7.5′quadrangle

see map on page 87

Introduction: A trip to Upper Galena Creek promises attractive views along the first part of the trip and beautiful snow-covered meadows at the climax. The relatively short distance coupled with the mellow grade of the access road produces a mild ascent suitable for beginners or for more experienced snowshoers limited to a half-day trip.

How to get there: From the Mt. Rose Summit descend westbound 0.3 mile to the trailhead at the beginning of the access road near a concrete block building, where you may find limited parking for a handful of cars on the westbound shoulder. If parking spaces are unavailable, descend another 0.5 mile on the highway to the Tahoe Meadows trailhead, where you will find a plowed parking area on the eastbound shoulder. On busy winter weekends the parking lot fills quickly, and you might be forced to park on the shoulder of the busy highway.

If you are coming from Incline Village, the Tahoe Meadows trailhead is 7.75 miles east of the junction between the Mt. Rose Highway and State Route 28.

Description: If you were able to park at the trailhead, follow the route of the access road as it climbs on a mild grade above the highway. Those parked at the Tahoe Meadows trailhead lot will have to cross the Mt. Rose Highway and make the short but steep climb up to the access road. At the road, scattered lodgepole pines allow for splendid views of both Tahoe Meadows and Incline Lake below and parts of Lake Tahoe farther west. Unfortunately, the lack of forest may also provide an unobstructed path for the winds that are common to the Mt. Rose area, resulting in wind-packed snow and chilling breezes.

Hike above the access road for about a mile, proceeding west until curving north, leaving the views behind as you enter light forest. Another 1.5 miles of mild ascent lead to the junction of the access road and an old section of the Mt. Rose Trail. Without a beaten path on the ground, this junction may not be obvious at first, particularly if the directional signs that guide summer visitors are buried by the winter snowpack.

Leaving the road, the route quickly ascends a low saddle and then drops into the upper basin of the Galena Creek drainage. Traverse around the head of the basin across the main channel of the creek to groves of lodgepole pine, which provide a pleasant locale for a winter picnic and for admiring the beauty of the basin and the snow-tinged cliffs above.

Some years ago, the upper basin of Galena Creek was threatened by the development of a destination resort, which would have blighted the beautiful scenery with condominiums and a casino. Fortunately, a land exchange was negotiated between the government and the owners of the property, protecting this marvelous resource.

To continue toward the summit of Mt. Rose, see Trip 21. Otherwise retrace your steps to the trailhead.

FYI: The open terrain, high elevation and prevailing winds produce cold temperatures, so dress accordingly. In addition, you most likely will experience hard-packed snow conditions in the wind-prone areas.

Warm-ups: Since the unfortunate closing of the Christmas Tree restaurant, winter recreationists traveling the Mt. Rose Highway must descend all the way toward the western outskirts of Reno to fine a decent eatery or watering hole. Those in search of a cocktail or an upscale dinner can stop at Sierra Solitaire Restaurant and Bar, 4 miles west of the U.S. 395 junction. Open Tuesday through Sunday, diners savor scrumptious entrees like wild salmon steak Vouvray, or lamb loin en croute chef Mordhorst. Call (775) 849-2100 for reservations. To view a menu, check out the website at **www.sierrasolitairerestaurant.com**.

TRIP 25

Relay Peak

Duration: Three-quarter day
Distance: 9 miles round trip
Difficulty: Moderate
Elevation: 8835/10338
Map: *Mt. Rose* 7.5' quadrangle

see map on page 87

Introduction: This popular mountain-bike road makes an excellent snow-shoe trip in winter. You may encounter cross-country skiers on their way to Galena Creek, particularly on a weekend, but most of them will be left behind at the base of Relay Ridge. The grade of the route is mild for most of the trip, increasing only for the final ascent to the ridge crest and the summit. Fine views of Lake Tahoe and the Tahoe Meadows area greet you from the top of Relay Ridge and the summit of Relay Peak.

How to get there: From Reno, travel south on U.S. 395 to the Mt. Rose Highway, State Route 431. Head west on S.R. 431 to Mt. Rose Summit, at 8900 feet the highest winter-maintained road in the Sierra. From the summit descend 0.3 mile to the trailhead at the beginning of the access road near a concrete block building, where you may find limited parking for a handful of cars on the westbound shoulder. If parking spaces are unavailable, descend another 0.5 mile on the highway to the Tahoe Meadows trailhead, where you will find a plowed parking area on the eastbound shoulder. On busy winter weekends the parking lot fills quickly, and you might be forced to park on the shoulder of the busy highway.

If you are coming from Incline Village, the Tahoe Meadows trailhead is 7.75 miles east of the junction between the Mt. Rose Highway and State Route 28.

Description: If you were able to park at the trailhead, follow the route of the access road as it climbs on a mild grade above the highway. Those parked at the Tahoe Meadows trailhead lot will have to cross the Mt. Rose Highway and make the short but steep climb up to the access road. At the road, scattered lodgepole pines allow for splendid views of both Tahoe Meadows and

Incline Lake below and parts of Lake Tahoe farther west. Unfortunately, the lack of forest may also provide an unobstructed path for the winds that are common to the Mt. Rose area, resulting in wind-packed snow and chilling breezes.

Hike above the access road for about a mile, proceeding west until curving north, leaving the views behind as you enter light forest. Another 1.5 miles of mild ascent lead to the junction of the access road and the old Mt. Rose Trail. Without a beaten path on the ground, this junction may not be obvious at first, particularly if the directional signs that guide summer visitors are buried by the winter snowpack.

Continue to follow the more obvious route of the access road as you head west. After one-third mile the road curves around to the base of the tramway serving the microwave station above on Relay Ridge. At this point you have the option of following the tramway straight up the steep slope directly to the ridge crest or continuing to follow the easier grade of the road.

If you don't mind the steep ascent and the slope is stable, you can reach the crest of Relay Ridge by gaining 400 vertical feet in 0.25 mile. Otherwise, continue on the road for another mile, gaining the same elevation in four times the distance. If you chose the route of the road, head south-southwest for 0.5 mile until doubling back to the north for the final 0.5 mile to the ridge crest.

From the top of Relay Ridge you have fine views of the Mt. Rose area and a part of Lake Tahoe. Once you have gained the ridge, head south-southwest along the ridge toward the summit of Relay Peak. After a half-mile you stand atop the summit of the peak, which in summer is the highest point along the entire Tahoe Rim Trail. The views from Relay Peak are stunning, with clear days allowing a vista that may extend all the way north to Mt. Shasta. Return the way you came.

FYI: At these elevations the winds may be nearly as fierce as on the summit of Mt. Rose, so be prepared.

Warm-ups: Since the unfortunate closing of the Christmas Tree restaurant, winter recreationists traveling the Mt. Rose Highway must descend all the way toward the western outskirts of Reno to fine a decent eatery or watering hole. Those in search of a cocktail or an upscale dinner can stop at Sierra Solitaire Restaurant and Bar, 4 miles west of the U.S. 395 junction. Open Tuesday through Sunday, diners savor scrumptious entrees like wild salmon steak Vouvray, or lamb loin en croute chef Mordhorst. Call (775) 849-2100 for reservations. To view a menu, check out the website at **www.sierra-solitairerestaurant.com**.

TRIP 26

Mt. Rose Highway to Lake Vista

see map on page 108

Duration: One-half day
Distance: 1.75-mile loop
Difficulty: Easy
Elevation: 8150/8430
Map: *Mount Rose* 7.5′ quadrangle

Introduction: This short and easy trip is a fine choice for a morning or afternoon excursion when you have only a couple of hours to spare, or you're looking for the bonus of a good lake view requiring minimal effort to get there. While hundreds may be cavorting around Tahoe Meadows a short drive away, this route is far less used and offers a chance for solitude that certainly will be lacking in the meadows.

How to get there: Find the starting point on the east shoulder of the Mt. Rose Highway (State Route 431), 3 miles southwest of the highway summit. Look for a plowed section of the shoulder near a highway gate and an electronic sign that is used to close the route during inclement weather conditions.

Description: From the parking area you make a brief ascent of a steep hillside to more level terrain and traverse through moderate forest cover to a rock outcropping, 0.5 mile from the road, from where you're treated to a stunning view of Lake Tahoe.

After admiring the view, you can simply retrace your steps back to the car, or follow the loop trip by heading northeast through the forest to the top of Peak 8430. From the top proceed north along the ridge to a saddle and an intersection with a snow-covered road. Turn left (northwest) and follow the road briefly to where it curves northeast. Leave the road and continue your northwest course for a short distance to another road that parallels the Mt. Rose Highway. Turn left (southwest) and follow this road and adjacent power line on a gradually increasing descent. Nearing the highway, the

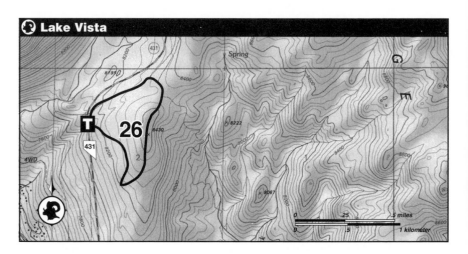

road curves to the right, but you should proceed ahead, following the continuation of the power line, soon reaching the parking area.

FYI: While the terrain is gentle and the navigation straightforward, the route is almost entirely in the trees, so some routefinding is required.

Warm-ups: The Galena Market at the corner of Thomas Creek Road and Mt. Rose Highway on the southeastern outskirts of Reno has long been a supporter of outdoor pursuits. Snowshoes are available for rent at $10 per day plus refundable deposit. In addition to the usual convenience store items, the establishment has a small snack bar with booth and counter seating, serving a variety of breakfast items, cold sandwiches, and hot snacks, including pizza slices, chicken strips, and burritos. The café is open from 6:30 A.M. to 2 P.M. daily.

CHAPTER 6

EAST TAHOE

The east shore of Lake Tahoe is perhaps the least developed side of the lake. Unfortunately, the relative lack of development doesn't necessarily translate into an abundant number of trips for snowshoers. The topography, composed of the thin spine of the Carson Range, which rises quickly from the lakeshore and then just as quickly plunges east towards the Carson Valley, limits the available acreage for recreational purposes.

Lake Tahoe Nevada State Park administers a fair portion of these limited recreational lands, where a cross-country ski concessionaire holds a permit for over 80 kilometers of groomed trails and a pair of backcountry cabins. Paying the park's $6 entrance fee allows snowshoers to use the area, provided they stay off the groomed ski trails. Trip 28 around Spooner Lake is within the park.

Some land on the east side of Tahoe is not in effect off-limits to snowshoers, but you may want to avoid these areas anyway. South of Highway 50 at Spooner Summit, a snowmobile concession launches a plethora of motorized madness on the slopes toward Daggett Pass, potentially spoiling an otherwise splendid 10-mile trip along the east crest of the Tahoe Basin. Farther south, Heavenly Valley Ski Resort covers the most acreage of any downhill ski area in the Lake Tahoe region. Besides the lack of access, a vast part of the east side of Tahoe either is off-limits to snowshoers or has its splendid qualities considerably diminished by other factors.

While the east side of Lake Tahoe has some drawbacks, the trips in this guide may be some of the finest around the lake. A spectacular view awaits the diligent traveler atop Snow Valley Peak on a little-used route from Spooner Summit, which generally follows the alignment of the Tahoe Rim Trail. Excellent views and a relative lack of use are just two of the many attributes waiting to be discovered in the east Tahoe area.

TRIP **27**

Snow Valley Peak

see map
on page
111

Duration: Full day
Distance: 9.5 miles round trip
Difficulty: Difficult
Elevation: 7145/9214
Maps: *Glenbrook & Marlette Lake* 7.5′ quadrangles

Introduction: Scenic beauty, reasonably dependable weather, and a location close to millions of people combine to make Lake Tahoe a popular winter playground. Finding a trip that offers a fair expectation of solitude can be difficult, especially on a weekend. The trip to Snow Valley Peak, generally following a segment of the Tahoe Rim Trail, may be just the ticket for escaping the masses. The price of that ticket, however, is a fairly strenuous trip requiring constant navigational skills. Over the first 3 miles you must negotiate your way through thick forest, without the aid of a marked route. In addition, you are likely to have to set your own trail, as the area sees little use. Therefore, this is a trip for experienced snowshoers only.

Although most of the trip is viewless, the climax of the ascent to Snow Valley Peak offers one of the most spectacular vistas of Lake Tahoe in the entire basin. From the 9214-foot summit, the entire lake lies at your feet. The basin-and-range topography of Nevada sprawls out to the east as well.

How to get there: Follow U.S. Highway 50, 0.75 mile east from the junction with State Route 28 near Lake Tahoe, or 9 miles west from the junction with U.S. Highway 395 in Carson City, to Spooner Summit. Park your vehicle in the plowed area on the north side of the highway, which serves as a Tahoe Rim trailhead in the summer.

Route description: The ideal path would be to proceed along the TRT all the way to Snow Valley Peak, but unless you are very familiar with the route it would be extremely difficult to follow, as it is not marked for winter travel. After a short climb away from the highway, you contour around forested hillsides well above Spooner Lake. Once beyond the vicinity of the lake,

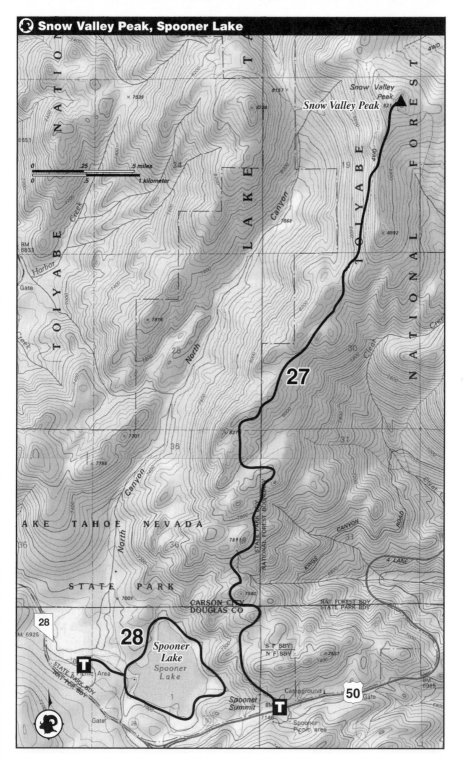

climb along a north compass bearing through the trees as you work your way toward the ridge crest above North Canyon on your left.

While not impossible, finding the most efficient way over and around the various buttes and high points along the ridge is made difficult by the thick woodlands. Due to the infrequent use this route receives, chances are you won't have much help from the tracks of previous visitors. Although some elevation loss is inevitable, minimize the decline while maintaining a general ascent in a northward direction. Rarely, the trees may thin just enough to allow you to see a part of Lake Tahoe to the west or Carson Valley to the east, affording you a brief opportunity to gain your bearings.

After 3 miles of travel amid mixed forest of pine and fir, you arrive at the base of the final ridge leading up to Snow Valley Peak. Begin an angling ascent along the west side of the ridge as the trees begin to thin. Soon you forget the miles of viewless climbing as a panoramic view of Lake Tahoe spreads out before you. The waters of Emerald Bay and Fallen Leaf Lake shimmer below the peaks of Desolation Wilderness on the far shore.

Continue to climb across the moderately steep slopes to the saddle separating Snow Valley Peak and Peak 8992, where the open slopes may be subject to wind-packed snow conditions. From the saddle ascend the final slope to the summit, where a truly awe-inspiring vista awaits. If the day is a pleasant one, you should be able to spy cross-country skiers below you along the groomed trail in North Canyon on their way to Marlette Lake.

After enjoying the view, retrace your steps back to Spooner Summit.

FYI: While you may be alone trudging along the Tahoe Rim Trail, each weekend hundreds of cross-country skiers use the groomed trails directly to the west around Spooner Lake and up North Canyon to Marlette Lake. If you decide to alter your return by descending the road from Snow Valley Peak and following the canyon back to the highway, be prepared to cough up

Tahoe from Snow Valley Peak

$16.50 to $21 (depending on the day) at Spooner Lake for a pass. For more information you can view the website at **www.crosscountryskitahoe.com.**

Warm-ups: There's nowhere close to the trailhead where snowshoers can grab a refreshing drink or a hot meal after their trip. However, farther westbound on Highway 50 is the Zephyr Cove Resort, a classic Tahoe landmark offering a wide range of dishes for breakfast, lunch, and dinner. The famous milkshakes are repeatedly voted as the best ones at the south end of the lake. In addition to the restaurant and full service bar, the resort offers additional services including lodging and cruises of Lake Tahoe. Call (800) 238-2463 for more information.

T R I P 28

Spooner Lake

Duration: One-half day
Distance: 2-mile loop
Difficulty: Easy
Elevation: 7000 (negligible change)
Map: *Glenbrook* 7.5' quadrangle

see map on page **111**

Introduction: Spooner Lake was created in the 1850s for use as a millpond and the dam was rebuilt in 1929 for irrigation purposes. Nowadays, recreation has replaced logging and irrigation as the principal activity within Lake Tahoe Nevada State Park, as people flock to the area in summer to hike, mountain bike, picnic, swim, bird watch, and fish. A large number of folks come in winter as well, primarily to cross country ski along the 80-plus kilometers of groomed trails. Without having to cough up the dough for a trail pass, although they will have to pay the $6 per day entrance fee, snowshoers can enjoy the loop around the lake alongside the skiers. However, snowshoers must absolutely stay out of the set tracks of the groomed trails.

The nearly 2-mile loop around the lake is a great trip for beginners, as the terrain is as flat as it comes, routefinding is not necessary alongside the marked ski trails, and the scenery is quite pleasant. The minimal distance and gentle terrain combine to make Spooner Lake a good choice for a short morning or afternoon trip.

How to get there: Drive on State Route 28 to the entrance into the Spooner Lake section of Lake Tahoe Nevada State Park, 1 mile northwest of the junction with Highway 50. Follow the park access road to the parking area.

Description: From the parking area, head east toward Spooner Lake. Proceed across the outlet stream and begin a clockwise loop around the lake. If the snowpack is light, you may be able to gain some information about the natural history of the area from several interpretive signs placed around the lake for summertime visitors. A forest of lodgepole pines, white firs, and Jeffrey pines rims the east side of the lake, while a large stand of aspens appears along the inlet near the southeast shore. Continue around the lakeshore and then head back to the parking area.

FYI: Since the park contains over 13,000 acres of Carson Range backcountry, additional snowshoe opportunities are quite numerous.

Warm-ups: Mountain bike champion Max Jones operates two backcountry cabins, Spooner and Wildcat, within the park that are open year round. The cabins are hand-hewn Scandinavian style structures that sleep 4–6 adults. The cabins are furnished with heating and cooking stoves, kitchen supplies, and odor-free composting toilets. Check out the website at **www.theflumetrail.com/cabins** for more information, or to make a reservation.

TRIP **29**

Castle Rock

Duration: One-half day
Distance: 2.5 miles round trip
Difficulty: Moderate
Elevation: 7800/7550/7900
Map: *South Lake Tahoe* 7.5' quadrangle

see map
on page
115

Introduction: This short trip would be rated as easy if not for the final scramble required to reach the top of Castle Rock and an inspiring view of Lake Tahoe. Requiring only a slight bit of navigation, the mostly forested route follows the course of a snow-covered road down the drainage of Burke

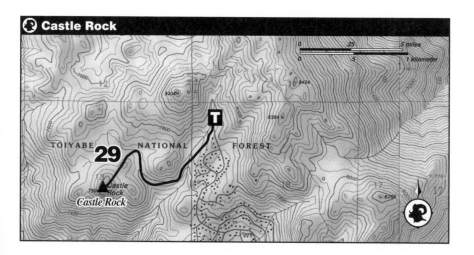

Castle Rock

Creek and then on a rising traverse to a saddle, where snowshoers leave the road behind for a short moderate climb to the base of the rocks. To reach the actual top of Castle Rock requires climbing skills, but a less ambitious scramble of some lower rocks will be rewarded with a stunning view of Lake Tahoe equal to one from the true summit. Although the distance is short and the navigation fairly straightforward, the scramble requires negotiation of steep snow ramps and high-angled rock and makes this a trip for experienced snowshoers only. The less ambitious might be satisfied with a view of Carson Valley and surrounding ranges to the east from the base of the rocks.

How to get there: Follow Highway 207 (Kingsbury Grade) to North Benjamin Drive, which is 2.9 miles east of the Highway 50 junction and 0.3 mile west of Daggett Pass, and turn north. North Benjamin Drive soon becomes Andria Drive, on which you continue to the end of the plowed road, 1.75 miles from Highway 207. Park your vehicle on the shoulder as space allows, obeying the sign to stay out of the snowplow turnaround.

Description: From the parking area, parallel the road for a short distance to where a snow-covered road (FS 13N80) heads downstream through the drainage of Burke Creek. Make a mild descent down the drainage amid a mixed forest of Jeffrey pines, lodgepole pines, and white firs for a half mile until the road veers away from the creek on a slightly rising traverse around the base of a hill to your right. Continue the mild ascent north to a broad, forested saddle northeast of Castle Rock.

A mile from the trailhead, you leave the road in the saddle and strike a southwest course that climbs more steeply toward Castle Rock, passing a subsidiary knob on the left along the way. The grade increases even more on the approach to the base of the rocks, where moderate forest cover inhibits any decent views of Lake Tahoe to the west.

To reach the actual summit of Castle Rock will require third or fourth class climbing skills. However, unobstructed views of Lake Tahoe are available from the slightly lower rocks to the left of the summit block requiring a slightly less daunting scramble up snow ramps and moderately angled slabs. A successful ascent reveals Tahoe in all her glory, with Marla Bay just to the right of Round Hill and the Crystal Range peaks glistening above the far shore. For those who may be intimidated by the scramble up the rocks for the lake vista, the area around the base of the rocks offers eastward views of the Carson Valley and ranges beyond.

FYI: You can minimize your encounters with snowmobiles in this area by taking this trip on a weekday, when the majority of the noisy, smog-belching beasts are stowed away at home. Even on weekends most of the traffic is left behind at the trailhead, as snowmobilers generally head northbound toward the slopes of Genoa and South Camp peaks. A few others seem to travel down Burke Creek, but even those seem to disappear where the snowshoe route leaves the drainage and heads toward Castle Rock.

Warm-ups: Head toward the lake on Highway 207 and then go eastbound on Highway 50 to the Zephyr Cove Resort, a classic Tahoe landmark offering a wide range of dishes for breakfast, lunch, and dinner. The famous milkshakes are repeatedly voted as the best ones at the south end of the lake. In addition to the restaurant and full service bar, the resort offers additional services including lodging and cruises of Lake Tahoe. Call (800) 238-2463 for more information.

Lake Tahoe from Castle Rock

CHAPTER 7

SOUTH TAHOE

To some, mention of the south shore of Lake Tahoe conjures up visions of opulent hotel-casinos, excessive commercialism, and traffic jams, an accurate portrayal of parts of the area. But, beyond the excessive visual stimulation, the crush of tourists, and the accompanying noise, the back-country near this end of the lake is perhaps the most dramatic and awe-inspiring piece of topography in northern California. Certainly, if history had been different and there had been no Comstock Lode in the 1800s to fuel the fires of development, a Lake Tahoe National Park would seem a reasonable possibility. The spectacular mountain scenery around the southern reaches of the lake would have provided a profound punctuation point to just such an idea.

South Tahoe as described in this guide encompasses the landscape around some of the highest passes in the area—Carson Pass, Luther Pass, and Echo Summit. The relatively high elevations around these passes provide access to some of the best snow conditions to be found anywhere around the lake, providing a long snowshoe season as well. This arbitrary division also includes the region around beautiful Fallen Leaf Lake, since access is primarily from the south due to periodic closures of Highway 89 around Emerald Bay due to the possibility of avalanches. Contained within this division are some of Tahoe's highest peaks and most dramatic mountain scenery. Two federal wilderness areas, Desolation and Mokelumne, lie in this part of the Tahoe backcountry.

Because of the rugged nature of the terrain, many of the trips in this section are rated as moderate or difficult. However, Scott Lake, Big Meadow, Angora Lookout, and Fallen Leaf Lake are rated as easy or have easy sections that beginners should feel comfortable snowshoeing. At the other end of the spectrum, ascents of Mt. Tallac, Waterhouse Peak, and Thompson Peak should challenge even the most technically advanced snowshoer. Nearly a dozen other trips fill in the middle of the range of difficulty. If you are interested in extending your wanderings beyond the descriptions, or considering an overnight stay in the backcountry, the south Tahoe region provides plenty of opportunities.

Carson Pass, Meiss Meadow, Echo Lakes, and Taylor Creek Sno-Parks provide developed access and parking for a number of trails described in this section. Other trailheads have extremely limited parking opportunities, some of which will require some creative parking solutions if there are more than a few cars in search of the little available space. If you have the luxury of a mid-week trip, parking should be less of a concern at most locations.

Whether you are searching for rugged peaks, cirque lakes, incomparable vistas, or challenging ascents, the south Tahoe region has them all. Any lover of mountains will develop a fond appreciation for the topography of this region.

Crystal Range from Waterhouse Peak

TRIP **30**

High Meadows & Star Lake

Duration: Three-quarter day to full day
Distance: 6.5 to 11 miles round trip
Difficulty: Moderate-Difficult
Elevation: 6525/7775; 6525/9125
Map: *Freel Peak* 7.5′ quadrangle

see map on page **120**

Introduction: High Meadows is a picturesque clearing above the southeast shore of Lake Tahoe in the shadow of Freel Peak (the Tahoe Basin's highest summit at 10,881 feet) and Jobs Sister (10,823′). Before the relatively recent construction of the Tahoe Rim Trail, the dirt road to High Meadows provided the sole access to isolated and lovely Star Lake. Unfortunately, that road crossed private property and was off limits to public access, leaving the meadows and the lake inaccessible to recreationists. In 2003 the Giovacchini family of Carson Valley sold a 1790-acre tract of land containing High Meadows to the Forest Service via the American Land Conservancy. Nowadays snowshoers, skiers, hikers, mountain bikers, and equestrians can legally travel along the road to High Meadows and beyond to Star Lake.

The road into High Meadows is moderately graded and easy to follow, providing snowshoers a straightforward route through dense forest to a series of clearings along Cold Creek. The meadows provide an excellent destination for groups seeking a relatively short (3.25 miles) trip with a minimum of elevation gain (1250′) that requires only a modicum of routefinding.

Star Lake is a highly scenic body of water cradled into an impressive cirque backdropped by the imposing north face of Jobs Sister. At an elevation of 9125 feet, Star is the highest lake within the Tahoe Basin—technically Mud Lake in the Mt. Rose Wilderness is about 140 feet higher, but it lacks any inlet or outlet and is really more of a pond than a bona fide lake. While the scenery is grand, reaching the lake is not easy considering the distance

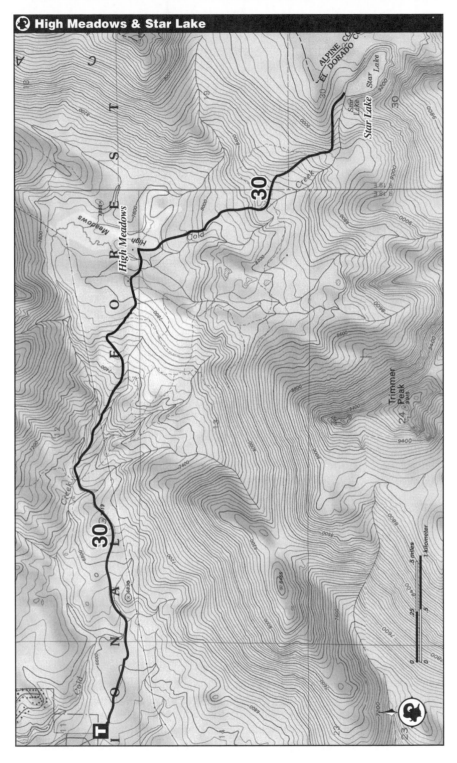

involved, the difficult terrain that must be negotiated along the way, and the need for a certain degree of routefinding beyond High Meadows. Therefore, this trip is recommended only for experienced backcountry travelers in good shape. For those who are up to the challenge, the beautiful lake and surroundings are a fine reward.

How to get there: From the intersection of U.S. 50 in South Lake Tahoe, drive on Pioneer Trail for 3.2 miles (4.5 miles from Highway 50/89 in Meyers) and turn onto High Meadows, which is just northeast of Sierra House Elementary School. Follow High Meadows for 0.7 mile to the end of plowed road and park as space allows.

Description: Follow the continuation of the closed road on a very mild climb through a mixed forest. Cross a wood bridge spanning a tributary of Cold Creek at 0.75 mile, pass by a ramshackle cabin, and then start climbing a little more steeply beyond a small meadow. The road follows the course of a power line for a while before ascending to the top of a forested flat. From there, make a short descent to a pair of crossings over Cold Creek at 1.6 and 1.75 miles.

Beyond the creek crossings, make a steady climb up the nose of a forested ridge between twin channels of the creek. As you progress up the hillside, the forest parts just enough to allow a decent view of the south end of Lake Tahoe and the peaks of Desolation Wilderness above the southwest shore. Beyond the view, veer right where a secondary road follows a power line cut and proceed to a Y-junction, 3 miles from the trailhead.

Bear left at the junction and continue along the road past an old cabin. About 25 yards past the cabin is a T-junction, where you should turn right, quickly reaching the fringe of High Meadows. Within the meadows the exact course of the road is hard to distinguish, but it does continue to the crossing of the aspen-lined creek near the south end of the meadows.

As both the immediate course of the road and the route of the hiking trail farther on to Star Lake tends to become very difficult to discern, turn upstream and follow the more defined course of the Cold Creek drainage. Head up the left-hand side of the canyon through mixed forest with occasional views of Lake Tahoe behind you. Continue a steady ascent up the canyon to the frozen lake nestled into a picturesque cirque below the towering north face of Jobs Sister. The scenic shoreline around the lake affords excellent campsites for overnighters.

FYI: The Giovacchini family retained 490 acres of property near High Meadows, but an easement allows public access across the property via the road. Therefore stick to the course of the road as best you can while traveling through this area in winter.

The shore of Star Lake makes a fine base camp for peakbaggers looking to add any of the three major summits in the area to their list of ascents.

While Jobs Sister, Freel Peak, and Jobs Peak all require a strenuous climb, the routes are not technically challenging.

Warm-ups: The excessive commercialism of South Shore tends to crowd out good independent eateries and watering holes. However, you can obtain some decent Cal-Mex cuisine at Chevy's Fresh Mex Restaurant, Tahoe's only representative of the nation-wide chain. Located on the main drag at 3678 Lake Tahoe Boulevard, a meal at Chevy's will fire you up after a jaunt in the frozen backcountry. Call (530) 542-1741 for reservations or more information.

TRIP 31

Big Meadow

see map on page 123

Duration: One-half day
Distance: 1.75 miles round trip
Difficulty: Easy
Elevation: 7250/7550
Maps: *Echo Lake & Freel Peak* 7.5' quadrangles

Introduction: Striding across the smooth snow above Big Meadow while enjoying the delightful scenery is a perfect way to spend a morning or an afternoon, particularly for beginning snowshoers, but also for those more experienced in search of a mellow way to begin the season, or get in a quick trip. The initial ascent is soon forgotten once the grade eases and you begin to feast your eyes on the splendid surroundings. If you desire a greater challenge, check out the two routes from Big Meadow to Scotts Lake and Round Lake in Trips 32 and 33.

How to get there: Travel California 89 to the Big Meadow trailhead, 3.3 miles west of Luther Pass and 5 miles from its junction with Highway 50 near Meyers. A small plowed parking area is across from the trailhead on the north shoulder of the highway.

Description: From the highway, you climb moderately through a forest cover of pine and fir. Well above the aspen-lined creek on the right, the trail

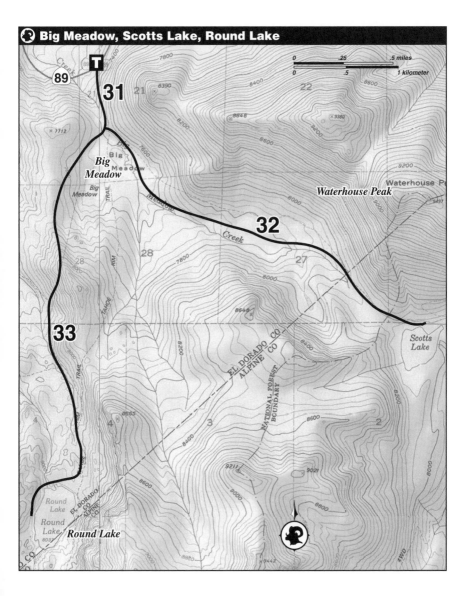

Big Meadow, Scotts Lake, Round Lake

weaves through the trees on a fairly discernible route up the drainage toward Big Meadow. After nearly a half-mile ascent, the grade gradually eases just before the meadow. Aptly named Big Meadow is a beautiful setting surrounded by dense forest and bisected by Big Meadow Creek. Beyond the far end of the clearing, rugged Waterhouse Peak rises above the surrounding topography. Big Meadow provides a perfect place for beginners to practice their stride and perfect their technique while enjoying the pleasant scenery. If you want to make a loop around the level terrain of the meadows, finding a convenient way across the creek and back may be necessary in order to complete the loop.

FYI: Parking is extremely limited, particularly on busy weekends, so you may want to arrive early to secure a space across from the trailhead. If the parking area is full, you will have to look around for space.

Warm-ups: If you're headed back toward South Lake Tahoe, consider dining at Passaretti's at 1381 Emerald Bay Road, 0.25 mile south of the Y on Highway 50/89. A former winner for best Italian restaurant in the annual "Best of Tahoe" poll conducted by the *Tahoe Daily Tribune*, Passaretti's serves traditional Italian fare at reasonable prices. Call (530) 544-6222 for reservations, or check out a menu at **www.passarettis.com**.

Big Meadow

TRIP **32**

Big Meadow Trailhead to Scotts Lake

see map
on page
123

Duration: Three-quarter day
Distance: 5.5 miles round trip
Difficulty: Moderate
Elevation: 7250/8080
Maps: *Echo Lake & Freel Peak* 7.5' quadrangles

Introduction: Enjoy a large meadow, a good-sized lake, and some excellent views of the Hope Valley and Carson Pass areas as you make the ascent along Big Meadow Creek to an 8000-foot pass. Basic navigation skills are required to negotiate the forested terrain, but, for those wishing to expand their skills, the straightforward nature of the topography on this trip provides a reasonably easy way to make the transition from marked trails to cross-country travel. (Merely 5.5 miles separate Highways 88 and 89 along this route; by utilizing a car shuttle you could avoid backtracking the 2.75 miles from the Big Meadow trailhead to Scotts Lake by reversing the description in Trip 41 and getting picked-up at the Scotts Lake trailhead on Highway 88.)

How to get there: Big Meadow Trailhead: Travel California 89 to the Big Meadow trailhead, 3.3 miles west of Luther Pass and 5 miles from its junction with Highway 50 near Meyers. A small plowed parking area is across from the trailhead on the north shoulder of the highway.

Description: From the highway, you climb moderately through a forest cover of pine and fir. Well above the aspen-lined creek on the right, the trail weaves through the trees on a fairly discernible route up the drainage toward Big Meadow. After nearly a half-mile ascent, the grade gradually eases just before the meadow where the routes to Scotts Lake and Round Lake (Trip 33) diverge. From the clearing you have a view of Waterhouse Peak, and your route to Scotts Lake proceeds along Big Meadow Creek to a pass directly south of the peak's summit. Head along the east edge of the meadow to the far end and work your way into the drainage of Big Meadow Creek.

Once you're away from the meadow and into the heavily forested drainage, try to stay a good distance up the side of the canyon, as the actual creek bottom is full of timber, deadfalls and brush. Continue to ascend the drainage toward the head of the canyon through the forested terrain. Approaching the saddle, the grade eases and the trees begin to thin enough to allow momentary views of Waterhouse Peak and the ridge on the opposite side of the canyon. Reach the saddle at 2.5 miles from the trailhead at an elevation of 8080 feet. To the west, the northeast face of Stevens Peak is particularly dramatic.

Just below the saddle lie the frozen waters of Scotts Lake, picturesquely placed below the steep flank of Stevens Peak. This enjoyable setting is a good location for an extended break or a lunch stop. After soaking in the surroundings, return the way you came to the Big Meadow trailhead. If you are feeling particularly ambitious and are in possession of the necessary skills, you could also ascend Waterhouse Peak (see Trip 42).

FYI: Parking is limited at Big Meadow trailhead.

Warm-ups: If you're returning via South Lake Tahoe, consider dining at Passaretti's at 1381 Emerald Bay Road, 0.25 mile south of the Y on Highway 50/89. A former winner for best Italian restaurant in the annual "Best of Tahoe" poll conducted by the *Tahoe Daily Tribune*, Passaretti's serves traditional Italian fare at reasonable prices. Call (530) 544-6222 for reservations, or check out a menu at **www.passarettis.com**.

Travelers on Highway 88 can dine on fresh-made dishes at Sorensen's Resort, one mile east of the Highway 88–89 junction. The charming café with a quaint mountain setting is open each day from 7:30 A.M. to 9 P.M. serving breakfast, lunch, and dinner. Dinner specialties include beef Burgundy stew, New York steak, and grilled salmon. In between meals patrons can drop by for a cup of hot chocolate, or a glass of beer or wine. In addition to the café, Sorensen's offers comfortable lodging in an assortment of mountain cabins. Call (800) 423-9949 to make a reservation. Check out their lodging packages at **www.sorensensresort.com**.

TRIP **33**

Big Meadow Trailhead to Round Lake

Duration: Three-quarter day
Difficulty: Moderate
Distance: 5.25 miles round trip
Elevation: 7275/8050
Maps: *Echo Lake, Freel Peak, & Caples Lake* 7.5' quadrangles

see map on page **123**

Introduction: When a fresh blanket of snow covers the environs of Round Lake, a setting more beautiful is hard to imagine. The circular lake is cradled beneath the striking cliffs of The Dardanelles, a volcanic formation that glistens in the sunlight after a dusting of light snow. Add in Big Meadow and a striking view of the Upper Truckee River drainage from the trip's high point and you have an unbeatable choice for a winter outing.

Trailhead: Travel California 89 to the Big Meadow trailhead, 3.3 miles west of Luther Pass and 5 miles from its junction with Highway 50 near Meyers. A small plowed parking area is across from the trailhead on the north shoulder of the highway.

Description: From the highway, you climb moderately through a forest cover of pine and fir. Well above the aspen-lined creek on the right, the trail weaves through the trees on a fairly discernible route up the drainage toward Big Meadow. After nearly a half-mile ascent, the grade gradually eases just before the meadow. Aptly named Big Meadow is a beautiful setting surrounded by dense forest and bisected by Big Meadow Creek.

From the near edge of the clearing, travel south across the meadow. After entering a covering of moderate forest, continue to bear south on a gradual ascent of the ridge west of the west branch of Big Meadow Creek. The grade increases as you draw near a forested pinnacle, 0.5 mile from Big Meadow. Pass below the pinnacle across the forested slopes on the east flank of the ridge and continue the ascent through lighter forest cover up to

Dardanelles and Round Lake

a pass separating the tributaries of Big Meadow Creek and the Upper Truckee River, 1.5 miles from the trailhead. At the pass you have decent views of Waterhouse Peak and the surrounding topography, and the view to the west of the Upper Truckee River country is quite impressive.

From the pass, make an angling descent across the steep hillside down to the bottom of the forested drainage. Proceed up the canyon, working your way over to the main channel of the creek that drains Round Lake. Following the creek, you eventually reach a steep slope just before the lake. Once you have surmounted this final incline, descend the short distance to the shoreline.

Round Lake is in an extraordinarily beautiful setting, under sheer volcanic cliffs above the east shore, known as The Dardanelles. These precipitous rock walls create a dramatic backdrop, well suited for a picnic lunch or a leisurely rest stop. If you have enough energy, you can extend your trip by climbing an additional 300 vertical feet in 1.25 miles to Meiss Lake.

From either Meiss or Round Lake retrace your steps to the trailhead.

FYI: This trip can be combined with Trip 46 for an 8-mile hike to Carson Pass, which would necessitate a car shuttle.

Warm-ups: If you're headed back toward South Lake Tahoe, consider dining at Passaretti's at 1381 Emerald Bay Road, 0.25 mile south of the Y on Highway 50/89. A former winner for best Italian restaurant in the annual "Best of Tahoe" poll conducted by the *Tahoe Daily Tribune*, Passaretti's serves traditional Italian fare at reasonable prices. Call (530) 544-6222 for reservations, or check out a menu at **www.passarettis.com**.

TRIP **34**

Grass Lake Meadow

see map
on page
129

Duration: One-half day
Distance: 0.5 to 3.75 miles
Difficulty: Easy
Elevation: 7700
Map: *Freel Peak* 7.5' quadrangle

Introduction: The Grass Lake area is a fine place for beginners to acquire a feel for the sport of snowshoeing. The flat terrain is easily negotiated and the openness of the meadow requires little in the way of navigation. Situated below the northeast slopes of Waterhouse Peak, the meadow is an attractive winter locale and would be an equally fine destination for more experienced snowshoers looking for a good place to kill an hour or two.

How to get there: Travel on California Highway 89 south from South Lake Tahoe or north from the junction with Highway 88 to Luther Pass. Park your vehicle in the plowed area at the pass along the highway shoulder.

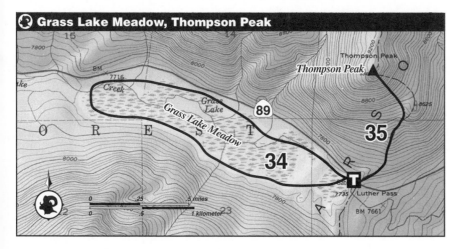

Grass Lake Meadow, Thompson Peak

Description: Ascend the snowbank at the parking area and stroll about the meadow in whatever direction you feel led. A small pocket of the meadow at the east end near Luther Pass is separated by a grove of trees from the much larger main section. A complete loop around the entire meadow is about 3.75 miles long.

FYI: If you're pumped up with extra energy and need an additional challenge, an ascent of Waterhouse Peak from Grass Lake Meadow is quite possible, and is actually not quite as steep as the ascent from Scotts Lake described in Trip 42.

Warm-ups: If you're returning via South Lake Tahoe, consider dining at Passaretti's at 1381 Emerald Bay Road, 0.25 mile south of the Y on Highway 50/89. A former winner for best Italian restaurant in the annual "Best of Tahoe" poll conducted by the *Tahoe Daily Tribune*, Passaretti's serves traditional Italian fare at reasonable prices. Call (530) 544-6222 for reservations, or check out a menu at **www.passarettis.com**.

Travelers on Highway 88 can dine on fresh-made dishes at Sorensen's Resort, one mile east of the Highway 88–89 junction. The charming café with a quaint mountain setting is open each day from 7:30 A.M. to 9 P.M. serving breakfast, lunch, and dinner. Dinner specialties include beef Burgundy stew, New York steak, and grilled salmon. In between meals patrons can drop by for a cup of hot chocolate, or a glass of beer or wine. In addition to the café, Sorensen's offers comfortable lodging in an assortment of mountain cabins. Call (800) 423-9949 to make a reservation. Check out their lodging packages at **www.sorensensresort.com**.

T R I P 35

Thompson Peak

see map
on page
129

Duration: One-half day
Distance: 1.5 miles round trip
Difficulty: Extreme
Elevation: 7730/9340
Map: *Freel Peak* 7.5' quadrangle

Introduction: Although the distance from the highway to the summit of Thompson Peak is a mere 0.75 mile, the terrain is exceedingly steep, gaining nearly 1600 feet. If the snow conditions near the summit are less than favorable, the ascent can be exceedingly difficult as well. Therefore, the short, steep climb to the summit is recommended for very experienced parties only.

The view from the summit is quite rewarding and worth the effort that the ascent entails. A multitude of peaks can be seen, from the Lake Tahoe region to beyond Carson Pass. Due to the difficult nature of the ascent, chances are you probably won't have to share the summit with anyone.

How to get there: Travel on California Highway 89 south from South Lake Tahoe or north from the junction with Highway 88 to Luther Pass. Park your vehicle in the plowed area at the pass along the highway shoulder.

Description: From the pass, begin snowshoeing directly up the steep slopes through a smattering of pines, fir, and quaking aspen. The best line of ascent is to follow just below the ridge crest. Continue to climb as the grade increases and the trees thin as you near the summit. The snow conditions on the upper part of the mountain may affect your mode of ascent; if you encounter hard-packed snow, removing your snowshoes may make the climb easier to negotiate.

The view from the summit is spectacular in all directions. Although you can't see Lake Tahoe from the top of Thompson Peak, your vista certainly does not lack for inspiring scenery. The peaks of Carson Pass and southern Tahoe as seen from the summit are almost too numerous to count.

FYI: If icy conditions are possible on the upper part of the trip, taking a pair of crampons and an ice ax would be a wise precaution.

Warm-ups: If you're returning via South Lake Tahoe, consider dining at Passaretti's at 1381 Emerald Bay Road, 0.25 mile south of the Y on Highway 50/89. A former winner for best Italian restaurant in the annual "Best of Tahoe" poll conducted by the *Tahoe Daily Tribune*, Passaretti's serves traditional Italian fare at reasonable prices. Call (530) 544-6222 for reservations, or check out a menu at **www.passarettis.com**.

Travelers on Highway 88 can dine on fresh-made dishes at Sorensen's Resort, one mile east of the Highway 88–89 junction. The charming café with a quaint mountain setting is open each day from 7:30 A.M. to 9 P.M. serving breakfast, lunch, and dinner. Dinner specialties include beef Burgundy stew, New York steak, and grilled salmon. In between meals patrons can drop by for a cup of hot chocolate, or a glass of beer or wine. In addition to the café, Sorensen's offers comfortable lodging in an assortment of mountain cabins. Call (800) 423-9949 to make a reservation. Check out their lodging packages at **www.sorensensresort.com**.

View from Thompson Peak

TRIP **36**

Horse Meadow

see map
on page
134

Duration: Three-quarter day
Distance: 8.5 miles round trip
Difficulty: Moderate
Elevation: 7480/8520
Map: *Freel Peak* 7.5' quadrangle

Introduction: A pleasant hike along a mildly graded road leads to Horse Meadow. From the meadows you have a good view of the highest mountain in the Tahoe Basin, Freel Peak, at 10,881 feet. The area appears to receive light use, providing a reasonable opportunity for solitude.

How to get there: On Highway 89, go 1.7 miles north from the junction with Highway 88 or 0.75 mile south from Luther Pass, to Forest Road 051. Park your vehicle as space allows in the small plowed area on the north side of the highway at the beginning of the road. A very short distance up the road a closed gate blocks vehicle progress during the off-season.

Description: Begin a moderate ascent along the course of the road through a light, mixed forest of pine, fir, and some cedar. Initially, you have excellent views behind you of the area around Hope Valley. Soon the grade of the road abates and you hike along a mild course heading northeast, paralleling the ridgeline above. Remain on the main road, veering left at a couple of Y-junctions. Follow the road as it crosses a creek and heads toward a flat, nearly 2 miles from the trailhead.

Beyond the flat the actual course of the road may become hard to determine, but the routefinding is fairly straightforward: head northeast into the drainage of Willow Creek and follow the stream up the valley. Along the way the route passes through areas of aspens, moderately dense forest, and small meadows before reaching Horse Meadow, 4.25 miles from Highway 89.

Horse Meadow provides a pleasant destination, a slightly sloping open area ringed by pine and fir where you have a dramatic view of Freel Peak, 3300 feet above.

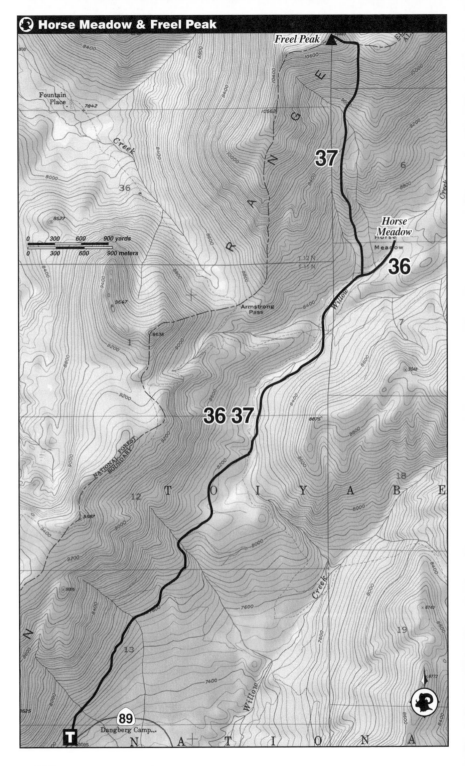

Freel Peak

37

Horse Meadow

36

Armstrong Pass

36 37

NATIONAL FOREST BOUNDARY

T O I Y A B E

Fountain Place

Creek

Willow

Willow

Creek

89

Dangberg Camp...

N A T I O N A

FYI: You may have to deal with snowmobilers along the road, although most of them seem to head toward Armstrong Pass.

Warm-ups: If you're returning via South Lake Tahoe, consider dining at Passaretti's at 1381 Emerald Bay Road, 0.25 mile south of the Y on Highway 50/89. A former winner for best Italian restaurant in the annual "Best of Tahoe" poll conducted by the *Tahoe Daily Tribune*, Passaretti's serves traditional Italian fare at reasonable prices. Call (530) 544-6222 for reservations, or check out a menu at **www.passarettis.com**.

Travelers on Highway 88 can dine on fresh-made dishes at Sorensen's Resort, one mile east of the Highway 88–89 junction. The charming café with a quaint mountain setting is open each day from 7:30 A.M. to 9 P.M. serving breakfast, lunch, and dinner. Dinner specialties include beef Burgundy stew, New York steak, and grilled salmon. In between meals patrons can drop by for a cup of hot chocolate, or a glass of beer or wine. In addition to the café, Sorensen's offers comfortable lodging in an assortment of mountain cabins. Call (800) 423-9949 to make a reservation. Check out their lodging packages at **www.sorensensresort.com**.

TRIP 37

Freel Peak

Duration: Full day
Distance: 11.5 miles round trip
Difficulty: Extreme
Elevation: 7480/10881
Map: *Freel Peak* 7.5' quadrangle

see map on page **134**

Introduction: The ascent of Freel Peak is a rigorous endeavor, but one that brings great rewards in the form of an unparalleled view from the summit as well as boasting rights for a winter ascent of Tahoe's highest peak. To reach the base of the mountain requires a 4.25-mile journey to Horse Meadow, a relatively easy trip gaining just over 1000 feet. From the meadow the grade becomes serious, ascending over 3300 feet in 1.5 miles. Even when snow conditions are favorable, this trip takes a full day and is best done late in the season when the days are longer.

If you are fortunate enough to reach the summit on a clear day, the vista will be magnificent. The entire lake spreads out below you in all its majesty, and the towering peaks above the shoreline sparkle in the glistening sun. Losing track of time while enjoying the magnificent view is a common occurrence. Unless the wind drives you from the summit, you must tear yourself away from the spectacular scenery before the day moves toward nightfall.

How to get there: On Highway 89, go 1.7 miles north from the junction with Highway 88 or 0.75 mile south from Luther Pass, to Forest Road 051. Park your vehicle as space allows in the small plowed area on the north side of the highway at the beginning of the road. A very short distance up the road a closed gate blocks vehicle progress during the off-season.

Description: Begin a moderate ascent along the course of the road through a light, mixed forest of pine, fir, and some cedar. Initially, you have excellent views behind you of the area around Hope Valley. Soon the grade of the road abates and you hike along a mild course heading northeast, paralleling the ridgeline above. Remain on the main road, veering left at a couple of Y-junctions. Follow the road as it crosses a creek and heads toward a flat, nearly 2 miles from the trailhead.

Tahoe near Freel Peak

Beyond the flat the actual course of the road may become hard to determine, but the routefinding is fairly straightforward: head northeast into the drainage of Willow Creek and follow the stream up the valley. Along the way the route passes through areas of aspens, moderately dense forest, and small meadows before reaching Horse Meadow, 4.25 miles from Highway 89.

From the meadow, climb up the bank above the east side of the creek draining the south side of Freel Peak. Continue to climb above the creek until you reach a mildly sloping basin around the 9300-foot level. At the head of the basin angle away from the drainage, following the most direct path to the saddle directly east of the summit of Freel Peak. Climb the steep slopes to the saddle through stunted whitebark pines and then turn west and follow the ridge to the top.

The view from the summit of Freel Peak is one of the finest in the entire Lake Tahoe region. The lake is seen in all its glory, the deep blue waters reflecting the hills and peaks above the shoreline. Across the lake, dominating the south end, is the dark hulk of Mt. Tallac. Just beyond Tallac, Pyramid Peak strikes an equally impressive profile, presiding over the Crystal Range and Desolation Wilderness. To the north is Mt. Rose, third highest peak in the Tahoe Basin at 10,776 feet. Nearby are Freel's companions, Jobs Sister, second highest peak at 10,823, and Jobs Peak farther east.

FYI: Due to the steep angle of ascent up the south slopes of Freel Peak and the potential for avalanches, this climb should be attempted only when snow conditions are stable.

Warm-ups: If you're returning via South Lake Tahoe, consider dining at Passaretti's at 1381 Emerald Bay Road, 0.25 mile south of the Y on Highway 50/89. A former winner for best Italian restaurant in the annual "Best of Tahoe" poll conducted by the Tahoe Daily Tribune, Passaretti's serves traditional Italian fare at reasonable prices. Call (530) 544-6222 for reservations, or check out a menu at **www.passarettis.com.**

Travelers on Highway 88 can dine on fresh-made dishes at Sorensen's Resort, one mile east of the Highway 88–89 junction. The charming café with a quaint mountain setting is open each day from 7:30 A.M. to 9 P.M. serving breakfast, lunch, and dinner. Dinner specialties include beef Burgundy stew, New York steak, and grilled salmon. In between meals patrons can drop by for a cup of hot chocolate, or a glass of beer or wine. In addition to the café, Sorensen's offers comfortable lodging in an assortment of mountain cabins. Call (800) 423-9949 to make a reservation. Check out their lodging packages at **www.sorensensresort.com.**

Grover Hot Springs State Park

see map
on page
139

Duration: One half day
Distance: 3 miles round trip
Difficulty: Easy
Elevation: 5825/6000
Map: *Markleeville* 7.5' quadrangle

Introduction: Grover Hot Springs State Park is a winter oasis off the beaten track. Even though it's open year round, the park is relatively quiet in the winter months, beckoning snowshoers and skiers to the open meadows and serene forests. The flat topography in the immediate vicinity near the park entrance provides easy snowshoeing—fine terrain for beginner and intermediate snowshoers. More advanced users can venture into more daunting terrain along Hot Springs and Charity Valley creeks. The main attraction to the area is the possibility of a soak in the hot springs after the trip (see Warm-ups below).

Parking is limited in the winter months, the hot springs are only open during certain hours, and the snow conditions at these elevations can be uncertain. Therefore, calling ahead to get the current information is a wise idea (see FYI).

How to get there: From the tiny community of Woodfords, drive south from the junction with Highway 88 on Highway 89 for about 7 miles to the town of Markleeville. Turn west from the center of town onto Hot Springs Road and proceed 3.5 miles to the park entrance. If you're not intending to visit the hot springs after your trip, park in the day use area ($6), otherwise follow signs to the hot springs parking lot.

Description: From either the day use or hot springs parking areas, head across the mostly open terrain bordering Hot Springs Creek and proceed up the valley. Eventually the meadows are left behind, as the route enters a for-

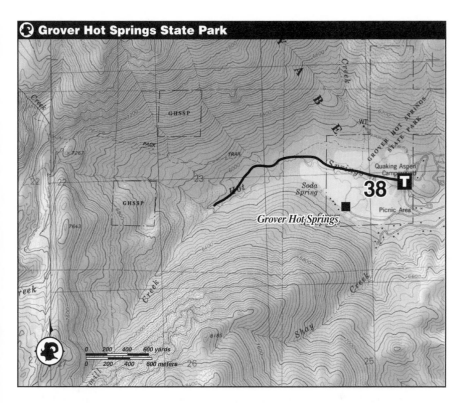

Grover Hot Springs State Park

est of junipers, firs, Jeffrey pines, and incense cedars. Past a small meadow the canyon narrows and the terrain becomes steeper, which is a good place for most groups to turn around. More experienced parties with good routefinding skills can continue up the canyon of Hot Springs Creek to Burnside Lake, or connect with Charity Valley Creek and follow it downstream to Charity Valley and Blue Lakes Road.

FYI: The relatively low elevation tends to influence the condition of the snowpack. Call ahead to the park, (530) 694-2248, to check the current conditions.

Warm-ups: Soaking in Grover Hot Springs provides an excellent way to conclude your snowshoe trip. The springs are open on weekends from 10 A.M. to 8 P.M. and during the week from 2 P.M. to 8 P.M., except on Wednesdays when the pool is closed. Fees are $5 for adults, $2 for kids. Call (530) 694-2249 for more information.

Hope Valley Overlook

see map
on page
141

Duration: Three-quarters day
Distance: 6 miles round trip
Difficulty: Moderate
Elevation: 6900/8100
Map: *Freel Peak* 7.5' quadrangle

Introduction: A marked ski route follows the course of a Forest Service road for 2.6 miles, followed by a 0.3-mile jaunt to the edge of a cliff and a fine overlook of Hope Valley and the surrounding terrain. A meal or a couple of nights at the nearby Sorensen's Resort would be the ideal compliment to the snowshoe trip (see Warm-ups below).

How to get there: Travel on California Highway 88 to Hope Valley, east of Carson Pass. Find a very small plowed parking area on the south shoulder of the highway, immediately west of Sorensens Resort, approximately 0.8 miles east of the junction with California Highway 89. Parking is extremely limited with room for only 3 to 4 cars at the trailhead. Another small plowed area on the opposite shoulder may have room for a similar number of vehicles.

Description: Away from the highway, you begin a winding climb that follows the course of a snow-covered road through a mixed forest of firs, pines, and aspens. Blue diamond markers will help keep you on route, as the road makes several switchbacks on the moderate to moderately steep ascent. After 0.75 mile of stiff climbing the grade eases for a while, but only for a brief time. The ascent resumes and leads to where the forest parts enough to allow a good view of Hope Valley and the surrounding peaks, about 1.75 miles from the highway, a hint at better views waiting above.

Soon back into forest, the road climbs 0.25 mile to a junction with a road from Deep Canyon to the east. Veer right (southwest) and follow a westward traverse through a mixed forest of western white pines, red and white firs, lodgepole pines, and junipers. At 2.6 miles, reaching a point directly

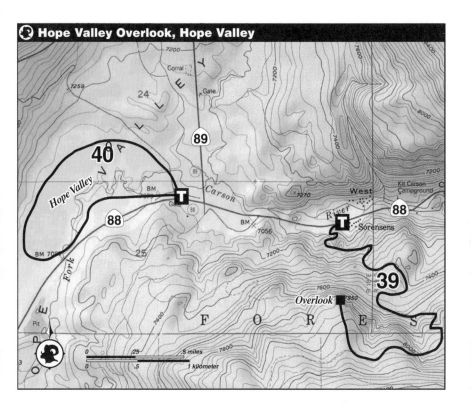

Hope Valley Overlook, Hope Valley

north of the summit of Pickett Peak, you turn north away from the road and make a gradual descent toward Point 7950.

Head north on a course that follows the right-hand side of a bench toward the edge of some cliffs southeast of Point 7950. After 0.3 mile, you stand at the edge of an overlook with excellent views of Hope Valley and the peaks near Luther Pass. More wide ranging views of the area can be obtained by continuing west 0.5 mile on the road and then heading north 0.1 mile to another overlook.

FYI: The marked ski route continues to follow FS Road 053 to Burnside Lake Road. From there, you could head either northwest on the road to a pickup point at Highway 88 near the junction with Highway 89, or travel southeast to Burnside Lake and then follow a more difficult and much longer route along the course of a hiking trail southeast to Charity Valley Creek and then east into Grover Hot Springs State Park. Another alternative trip extension would be a climb of 9118-foot Pickett Peak for an even more commanding view of the region.

Warm-ups: Travelers on Highway 88 can dine on fresh-made dishes at Sorensen's Resort, one mile east of the Highway 88–89 junction. The charming café with a quaint mountain setting is open each day from 7:30 A.M. to 9 P.M. serving breakfast, lunch, and dinner. Dinner specialties include beef Burgundy stew, New York steak, and grilled salmon. In between meals patrons can drop by for a cup of hot chocolate, or a glass of beer or wine. In addition to the café, Sorensen's offers comfortable lodging in an assortment of mountain cabins. Call (800) 423-9949 to make a reservation. Check out their lodging packages at **www.sorensensresort.com.**

TRIP **40**

Hope Valley

see map
on page
141

Duration: One-half day
Distance: 0.5 to 2.5 miles
Difficulty: Easy
Elevation: 7080
Map: *Freel Peak* 7.5' quadrangle

Introduction: Hope Valley offers gentle terrain without the need for much routefinding, a definite attraction for neophytes or more experienced groups in search of an easy trip. Surrounded by towering peaks, the expansive and open meadows offer plenty of good scenery as well. Don't expect much solitude on weekends.

How to get there: Travel on California Highway 88 to Hope Valley, east of Carson Pass. Park as space allows on the shoulder of the highway near the junction with California Highway 89.

Description: The flat, mostly open terrain of Hope Valley creates a fine area for snowshoers looking for a way to get introduced to the sport, or for more experienced snowshoers in search of less challenging conditions. The expansive meadows allow groups to tailor their trips to as long or as short as they choose. The surrounding peaks and ridges provide a fine scenic backdrop to the gentle terrain of Hope Valley.

FYI: The gentle slopes, easy access, and open terrain make Hope Valley a popular destination for a wide range of recreationists. Cross country skiers will usually be here in great numbers on weekends during good weather— remember to stay out of their ski tracks. Snowmobilers may also be present in significant numbers, although the majority seems to prefer the terrain south of the highway.

Warm-ups: Travelers on Highway 88 can dine on fresh-made dishes at Sorensen's Resort, one mile east of the Highway 88–89 junction. The charming café with a quaint mountain setting is open each day from 7:30 A.M. to 9 P.M. serving breakfast, lunch, and dinner. Dinner specialties include beef Burgundy stew, New York steak, and grilled salmon. In between meals patrons can drop by for a cup of hot chocolate, or a glass of beer or wine. In addition to the café, Sorensen's offers comfortable lodging in an assortment of mountain cabins. Call (800) 423-9949 to make a reservation. Check out their lodging packages at **www.sorensensresort.com**.

Hope Valley

TRIP 41

Scotts Lake

Duration: One-half day
Distance: 3 miles round trip
Difficulty: Easy
Elevation: 7115/8035
Map: *Freel Peak* 7.5' quadrangle

see map on page **145**

Introduction: The journey to Scotts Lake is a short, easy trip to a high mountain lake with spectacular views of the region east of Carson Pass.

How to get there: Travel on California Highway 88 to Hope Valley, east of Carson Pass. Find a small plowed parking area on the west shoulder of the highway, 1.5 miles west of the junction with California Highway 89.

Description: You could follow the marked ski trail that corresponds to the path of the winding road to Scotts Lake, but competent snowshoers can take a more direct approach by gaining a bearing on the low saddle in the ridge

Scotts Lake

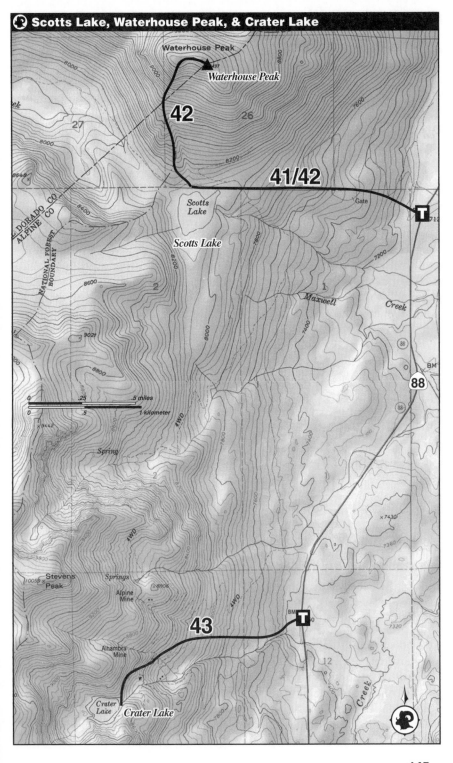

Scotts Lake, Waterhouse Peak, & Crater Lake

Waterhouse Peak

Waterhouse Peak

42

41/42

Scotts Lake

Scotts Lake

Gate

T

Maxwell

Creek

88

BM

88

El DORADO CO

ALPINE CO

NATIONAL FOREST BOUNDARY

Spring

4WD

Stevens Peak

Springs

Alpine Mine

4WD

Alhambra Mine

43

BM

T

Crater Lake

Crater Lake

Creek

just south of Waterhouse Peak, as Scotts Lake sits right below this saddle. From the highway, head on a westerly course across a flat and up the forested hillside. After a mile of moderate ascent, the grade eases just before you reach the lake. Scotts Lake provides an ideal setting for admiring the splendid scenery, particularly the rugged north face of Stevens Peak.

FYI: If you're looking for a spot to test your winter camping skills, Scotts Lake provides a pleasant setting not far from the highway.

Warm-ups: Travelers on Highway 88 can dine on fresh-made dishes at Sorensen's Resort, one mile east of the Highway 88–89 junction. The charming café with a quaint mountain setting is open each day from 7:30 A.M. to 9 P.M. serving breakfast, lunch, and dinner. Dinner specialties include beef Burgundy stew, New York steak, and grilled salmon. In between meals patrons can drop by for a cup of hot chocolate, or a glass of beer or wine. In addition to the café, Sorensen's offers comfortable lodging in an assortment of mountain cabins. Call (800) 423-9949 to make a reservation. Check out their lodging packages at **www.sorensensresort.com.**

TRIP 42

Waterhouse Peak

Duration: Three-quarters day
Distance: 5 miles round trip
Difficulty: Difficult
Elevation: 7115/9497
Map: *Freel Peak* 7.5' quadrangle

see map on page 145

Introduction: Absolutely gorgeous views of the northern Sierra are the chief reward for the steep climb to the summit of Waterhouse Peak. A clear day with little or no wind is the perfect time to attempt the peak. The degree of ascent and the potentially difficult snow conditions on the upper part of the mountain combine to make this trip one for experienced snowshoers only. Due to the high angle of the slopes, the climb should be made when the avalanche danger is minimal.

How to get there: Travel on California Highway 88 to Hope Valley, east of Carson Pass. Find a small plowed parking area on the west shoulder of the highway, 1.5 miles west of the junction with California Highway 89.

Description: You could follow the marked ski trail that corresponds to the path of the winding road to Scotts Lake, but competent snowshoers can take a more direct approach by gaining a bearing on the low saddle in the ridge just south of Waterhouse Peak, as Scotts Lake sits right below this saddle. From the highway, head on a westerly course across a flat and up the forested hillside. After a mile of moderate ascent, the grade eases just before you reach the lake.

From the lake, begin the steep climb up the forested south slopes of Waterhouse Peak. About half way up the mountain, the trees begin to thin, and eventually they all but disappear. The grade of the slope also increases a bit as you gain altitude. Above tree line, the snow conditions may become hard-packed, requiring a higher degree of skill and caution. Nearing what appears to be the top of the mountain, you reach a small plateau that must be crossed in order to reach the base of the summit rocks. Beyond the plateau, a short, steep climb completes the ascent.

Scott Lake from Waterhouse Peak

From the top of Waterhouse Peak, you are blessed with one of the most dramatic views in the Carson Pass area. To the south, a vast array of peaks presents itself—you could while away the hours trying to identify them all. Gazing toward Tahoe, you have a beautiful view of the lake as well as a dramatic presentation of the Crystal Range peaks of Desolation Wilderness. Nearby, the mountains surrounding Carson Pass seem close enough to reach out and touch.

FYI: Waterhouse Peak is a popular climb for advanced skiers in search of the perfect powder run. The snow on the peak's north slopes stays in good shape for long periods, attracting a sizable population of skiers on weekends. However, you should be alone on your side of the mountain, as the ski crowd follows the standard and much easier route from Luther Pass to the summit.

Warm-ups: Travelers on Highway 88 can dine on fresh-made dishes at Sorensen's Resort, one mile east of the Highway 88–89 junction. The charming café with a quaint mountain setting is open each day from 7:30 A.M. to 9 P.M. serving breakfast, lunch, and dinner. Dinner specialties include beef Burgundy stew, New York steak, and grilled salmon. In between meals patrons can drop by for a cup of hot chocolate, or a glass of beer or wine. In addition to the café, Sorensen's offers comfortable lodging in an assortment of mountain cabins. Call (800) 423-9949 to make a reservation. Check out their lodging packages at **www.sorensensresort.com.**

T R I P 43

Crater Lake

see map
on page
145

Duration: One-half day
Distance: 2.75 miles round trip
Difficulty: Moderate
Elevation: 7360/8595
Map: *Carson Pass* 7.5' quadrangle

Introduction: A short, but steep ascent leads to a beautiful lake nestled in a dramatic cirque basin. While hundreds of weekend recreationists may be cavorting on the slopes near Carson Pass just a few miles away, chances are that you and your party will remain relatively undiscovered on this trip, in spite of the minimal distance required to reach such a spectacular setting. Excellent views of the Hope Valley and Carson Pass areas occur on the open slopes below the lake.

How to get there: On California Highway 88 find a small plowed area on the west side of the highway, 4.4 miles east of Carson Pass and 4.1 miles west of the Highway 88–89 junction.

Description: Begin a moderately steep ascent just above the north bank of the creek that drains Crater Lake. Aiming for the low spot in the ridge above, located 0.85 mile southeast of Stevens Peak, you pass through a light forest, composed primarily of lodgepole and ponderosa pine with some white fir and an occasional cedar. Near the damp soils of the creek you will also find some quaking aspen.

As you continue the climb, the forest begins to thin allowing for nice views of the areas around Hope Valley and Carson Pass. Cross-country skiers tend to utilize a couple of roads that zigzag up the slope on opposite sides of the drainage, but snowshoers can assume a more direct approach up the moderately steep hillside. Near the head of the creek, the terrain becomes steeper, requiring that you make an angling traverse to gentler slopes along the creek just below the rim of the basin. Follow the creek on a mellow grade for 500 feet before climbing steeply again to the rim and then dropping down quickly to Crater Lake.

The lake is set in a spectacular amphitheater rimmed by steep rock walls midway between the summits of Stevens and Red Lake Peaks. From the lip of the basin you have great views of the surrounding peaks and valleys.

FYI: Venturing toward the steep walls at the head of the canyon above Crater Lake should be done only when snow conditions are stable.

Warm-ups: Travelers on Highway 88 can dine on fresh-made dishes at Sorensen's Resort, one mile east of the Highway 88–89 junction. The charming café with a quaint mountain setting is open each day from 7:30 A.M. to 9 P.M. serving breakfast, lunch, and dinner. Dinner specialties include beef Burgundy stew, New York steak, and grilled salmon. In between meals patrons can drop by for a cup of hot chocolate, or a glass of beer or wine. In addition to the café, Sorensen's offers comfortable lodging in an assortment of mountain cabins. Call (800) 423-9949 to make a reservation. Check out their lodging packages at **www.sorensensresort.com**.

TRIP **44**

Red Lake Peak

see map on page **153**

Duration: One-half day
Distance: 5 miles round trip
Difficulty: Moderate
Elevation: 8560/10,063
Maps: *Carson Pass & Caples Lake* 7.5' quadrangles

Introduction: Without mountaineering equipment and the ability to use it, the actual summit of Red Lake Peak may be beyond your grasp. However, an easily accessible high point only a stone's throw away is only a few feet below the true apex. Supreme views of Lake Tahoe and the mountainous terrain of Carson Pass are the chief rewards. The trip ascends open slopes for almost the entire route, providing pleasant scenery throughout.

Red Lake Peak holds the distinctive historical honor of being the first Sierra peak ascended by Caucasians, as well as providing a vista point for the first recorded view of Lake Tahoe. On February 14, 1844, John C. Fremont, with his cartographer Charles Pruess, reached the summit and recorded the following statement concerning the ascent and the view, "With Mr. Pruess, I ascended today the highest peak up to the right: from which we had a beautiful view of a mountain lake at our feet, about fifteen miles in length, and so entirely surrounded by mountains that we could not discover an outlet."

How to get there: The Meiss Meadow Sno-Park is 0.2 mile west of Carson Pass on the north side of Highway 88 (a portable toilet is nearby). You must possess a day permit ($5) or a yearly permit ($25) to legally park at a California Sno-Park.

Description: From the parking lot, head west, generally contouring along the slopes of the lightly forested hillside. As you curve into a minor drainage, head for the obvious saddle to the north. Climb across open slopes, reaching the saddle in little over a mile. The bare terrain allows striking views to the south of Round Top and the surrounding peaks and ridges of the Carson Pass area.

Turning northeast from the saddle, you begin an angling ascent across moderately steep, wide-open slopes below Red Lake Peak. Choose a line of ascent that leads to the upper slopes, curving beneath the first rock outcropping on the ridge above. Once beyond the outcropping, Red Lake Peak comes into view and you can assume a direct line toward the summit. Head for the high point on the rounded ridge directly south of the rocks that form the true summit. You may encounter difficult snow conditions on the windswept west slopes near the summit.

As from most of the high points in the Carson Pass area, the view from the summit of Red Lake Peak is quite dramatic. Lake Tahoe glistens in the winter sun surrounded by snow-capped peaks, including the Crystal Range in Desolation Wilderness. The immediate array of peaks and canyons around Carson Pass composes one of the most rugged landscapes anywhere in the Tahoe region.

FYI: Signs at the Sno-Park warn backcountry users about the possibility of blasting for avalanche control along the Highway 88 corridor. The potential danger occurs on the steep slopes above the highway southeast of the summit of Red Lake Peak. Avoid wandering off the route on the east side of the ridge. Contact the appropriate authorities regarding avalanche conditions.

Warm-ups: Rustic Kirkwood Inn boasts of being one of the first resorts to operate in the northern Sierra. Modern-day travelers can partake of freshly cooked dishes created with a local flair for breakfast, lunch, and dinner. The moderately priced establishment also has a full bar and an appetizer menu. Kirkwood Inn is on Highway 88, 0.4 mile west of Caples Lake.

Route to Red Lake Peak

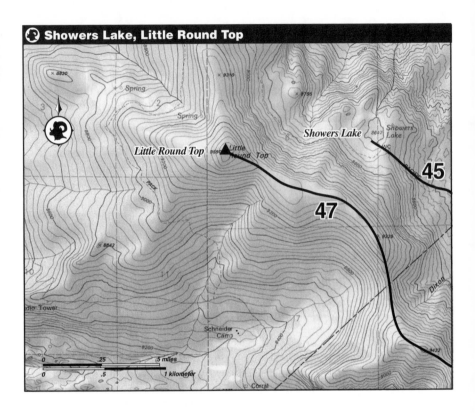

Showers Lake, Little Round Top

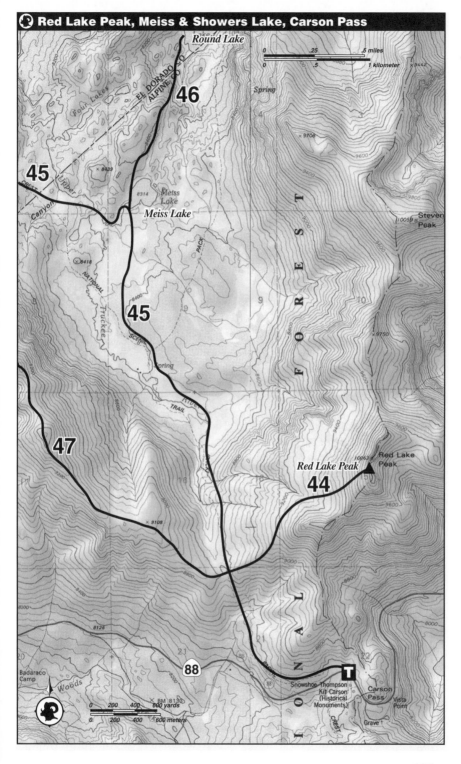

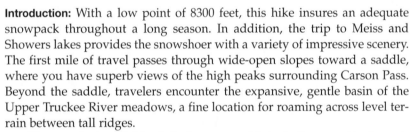

Meiss & Showers Lakes

see maps
on pages
152,153

Duration: Three-quarter day to Meiss Lake
Full day to Showers Lake
Distance: 7 miles round trip to Meiss Lake
10 miles round trip to Showers Lake
Difficulty: Moderate to Meiss Lake
Difficult to Showers Lake
Elevation: 8560/8315
8560/8795
Maps: *Carson Pass & Caples Lake* 7.5' quadrangles

Introduction: With a low point of 8300 feet, this hike insures an adequate snowpack throughout a long season. In addition, the trip to Meiss and Showers lakes provides the snowshoer with a variety of impressive scenery. The first mile of travel passes through wide-open slopes toward a saddle, where you have superb views of the high peaks surrounding Carson Pass. Beyond the saddle, travelers encounter the expansive, gentle basin of the Upper Truckee River meadows, a fine location for roaming across level terrain between tall ridges.

The round trip to Meiss Lake is a reasonable task, the ascent to the saddle being the only part requiring much effort. But, even though Showers Lake is just a little over a mile beyond Meiss Lake, reaching its scenic basin necessitates a fair climb.

How to get there: The Meiss Meadow Sno-Park is 0.2 mile west of Carson Pass on the north side of Highway 88 (a portable toilet is nearby). You must possess a day permit ($5) or a yearly permit ($25) to legally park at a California Sno-Park.

Description: From the parking lot, head west, generally contouring along the slopes of the lightly forested hillside. As you curve into a minor drainage, head for the obvious saddle to the north. Climb across open slopes, reaching the saddle in little over a mile. The bare terrain allows striking views to the south of Round Top and the surrounding peaks and ridges of the Carson Pass area

Leaving the saddle, which is the high point of your trip, a short, moderate descent north leads through a narrow drainage where large cornices may appear along the ridge crest to the west. If the sight of them makes you queasy, pick a descent route up the hillside on the east side of the drainage to avoid any possible avalanche run-out. Beyond the potential hazard, you encounter the gentle terrain of the expansive Upper Truckee River canyon. The nearly level gradient of the large basin provides easy snowshoeing as you follow the general course of the frozen river through widely scattered evergreens. The ridge to the west, which culminates at the summit of Little Round Top, provides a pleasant backdrop for the wide-open basin.

Even though the distance from the saddle to Meiss Lake is 2.5 miles, the gently descending grade along the Upper Truckee provides the illusion of a much shorter distance. The pleasant scenery seems to help you move quickly as you approach Meiss Lake.

Unless you are paying very close attention, it's easy to miss the lake, because the frozen body of water blends in perfectly with the flat floor of the basin, indistinguishable from the surrounding countryside. The lake is at the northeast end of a large clearing, just before some low hills blanketed with a dense covering of trees. The delightful scenery of the basin should more than compensate for anything lacking in the sight of the lake. The lake, 3.5 miles from the trailhead, is a worthy goal for most parties, particularly when you remember that the trip back to the saddle is uphill.

Heading toward the saddle on Meiss Lake Trail

If you want to push on toward Showers Lake, head west across the open basin and over the drainage of the Upper Truckee River into a more moderate forest cover. In order to reach the lake, you must leave the easy terrain of the basin and begin a healthy climb up a tree-covered hillside, eventually following a similar route to the Pacific Crest Trail as shown on the *Carson Pass* topo map. Continue the ascent until you crest the low ridge directly above the south shore. After a short drop, you reach picturesque Showers Lake, 1.25 mile from Meiss Lake and 5 miles from the Sno-Park.

From Showers Lake you can save a little distance on the return trip by heading straight back along the course of the Upper Truckee, avoiding the slight detour to Meiss Lake.

FYI: Check out Trip 46 for a challenging extension to this trip.

Warm-ups: Rustic Kirkwood Inn boasts of being one of the first resorts to operate in the northern Sierra. Modern-day travelers can partake of freshly cooked dishes created with a local flair for breakfast, lunch, and dinner. The moderately priced establishment also has a full bar and an appetizer menu. Kirkwood Inn is on Highway 88, 0.4 mile west of Caples Lake.

Meiss Lake Area

TRIP 46

Carson Pass to Round Lake

see map on page 153

Duration: Full day
Distance: 9.5 miles round trip
Difficulty: Difficult
Elevation: 8560/8795/8025
Maps: *Carson Pass & Caples Lake* 7.5' quadrangles

Introduction: This trip has many attractive features: a number of pleasant meadows, a spectacular lake rimmed by precipitous cliffs, and an awe-inspiring view of the high country around Carson Pass are just a few of the highlights. After climbing to a saddle from Carson Pass, the route passes through the tranquil meadows of the Upper Truckee River basin. Beyond the meadows, you encounter Round Lake at the base of The Dardanelles, a row of dramatic, vertical rock cliffs.

How to get there: Carson Pass Trailhead: The Meiss Meadow Sno-Park is 0.2 mile west of Carson Pass on the north side of Highway 88 (a portable toilet is nearby). You must possess a day permit ($5) or a yearly permit ($25) to legally park at a California Sno-Park.

Description: From the parking lot, head west, generally contouring along the slopes of the lightly forested hillside. As you curve into a minor drainage, head for the obvious saddle to the north. Climb across open slopes, reaching the saddle in little over a mile. The bare terrain allows striking views to the south of Round Top and the surrounding peaks and ridges of the Carson Pass area. The bare terrain provides striking views to the south of Round Top and the surrounding peaks and ridges of the Carson Pass area.

Leaving the saddle, which is the high point of your trip, a short, moderate descent north leads through a narrow drainage where large cornices may appear along the ridge crest to the west. If the sight of them makes you queasy, pick a descent route up the hillside on the east side of the drainage to avoid any possible avalanche run-out. Beyond the potential hazard, you encounter the gentle terrain of the expansive Upper Truckee River canyon. The nearly level gradient of the large basin provides easy snowshoeing as you follow the general course of the frozen river through widely scattered evergreens. The ridge to the west, which culminates at the summit of Little Round Top, provides a pleasant backdrop for the wide-open basin.

Even though the distance from the saddle to Meiss Lake is 2.5 miles, the gently descending grade along the Upper Truckee provides the illusion of a much shorter distance. The pleasant scenery seems to help you move quickly as you approach Meiss Lake.

Unless you are paying close attention, it's easy to miss the lake, because the frozen body of water blends in with the flat floor of the basin, indistinguishable from the surrounding countryside. The lake is at the northeast end of a large clearing, just before some low hills blanketed with trees.

From just beyond the north end of Meiss Lake follow the stream drainage that empties into Round Lake for 0.5 mile to an open meadow. Proceed along the east edge of the meadow until you reenter forest cover and then drop more steeply to the west side of Round Lake. The vertical cliffs known as The Dardanelles make an excellent reference point, as they form the east boundary of Round Lake's basin.

FYI: From the beautiful setting of Round Lake, you could reverse the route description in Trip 33 on a shuttle trip to the Big Meadow trailhead (see Trip 33). Be forewarned that this journey will tax your route-finding skills as you negotiate your way through moderate forest cover. The crux of the route-finding concerns is where to cross the ridge that separates the drainages of the Upper Truckee River and Big Meadow Creek. Head for the low point in the ridge, 0.4 mile north-northwest of Point 8665 on the topo map.

Warm-ups: If you're returning via South Lake Tahoe, consider dining at Passaretti's at 1381 Emerald Bay Road, 0.25 mile south of the Y on Highway 50/89. A former winner for best Italian restaurant in the annual "Best of Tahoe" poll conducted by the *Tahoe Daily Tribune*, Passaretti's serves traditional Italian fare at reasonable prices. Call (530) 544-6222 for reservations, or check out a menu at **www.passarettis.com**.

Travelers on Highway 88 can dine on fresh-made dishes at Sorensen's Resort, one mile east of the Highway 88–89 junction. The charming café with a quaint mountain setting is open each day from 7:30 AM to 9 PM serving breakfast, lunch, and dinner. Dinner specialties include beef Burgundy stew, New York steak, and grilled salmon. In between meals patrons can drop by for a cup of hot chocolate, or a glass of beer or wine. In addition to the café, Sorensen's offers comfortable lodging in an assortment of mountain cabins. Call (800) 423-9949 to make a reservation. Check out their lodging packages at **www.sorensensresort.com**.

TRIP **47**

Little Round Top

see maps
on pages
152, 153

Duration: Full day
Distance: 10.25 miles round trip
Difficulty: Moderate
Elevation: 8560/9590
Maps: *Carson Pass & Caples Lake* 7.5' quadrangles

Introduction: This little-known route to the summit of Little Round Top provides nearly continuous, awe-inspiring views. Beyond the first mile, the path follows an exposed ridge for another 4 miles, where snowshoers are continuously treated to some of the most fantastic scenery in the greater Lake Tahoe region. Even if you are short on time and unable to complete the entire trek, you could turn back at any point, satisfied with the extraordinary scenery.

The ridge route requires only minimal routefinding: gain the ridge and follow it to the end. In addition, the terrain is not particularly steep for any great distance, making this trip suitable for all but beginning snowshoers, provided they have the stamina for the journey.

How to get there: The Meiss Meadow Sno-Park is 0.2 mile west of Carson Pass on the north side of Highway 88 (a portable toilet is nearby). You must possess a day permit ($5) or a yearly permit ($25) to legally park at a California Sno-Park.

Description: From the parking lot, head west, generally contouring along the slopes of the lightly forested hillside. As you curve into a minor drainage, head for the obvious saddle to the north. Climb across open slopes, reaching the saddle in little over a mile. As you approach the saddle, bear left and ascend a moderately steep slope a short distance to the ridge crest. Follow the ridge over mild terrain until you reach the base of the first high point, where the slope becomes more moderate. Climb to the top of the high point, 1.75 miles from the trailhead, where you have excellent views of Round Top peak south across Highway 88 and of a part of Lake Tahoe to the north.

As you descend, the ridge bends slightly west, providing a chilling view of the nasty cornices that frequently appear on the east side of the ridge ahead. Obviously, you should avoid the extreme right-hand edge of the ridge near these cornices. Where the ridge narrows as it curves back toward the north, make a mildly ascending traverse over to the base of a significant peak. Then climb steeper slopes to the summit of the 9450-foot peak, 2.5 miles from the Sno-Park. As expected, the view from here is magnificent, including the meadows surrounding the Upper Truckee River immediately below you to the northeast as well as the snowy peaks around Carson Pass and Lake Tahoe.

Now descend moderate slopes 0.25 mile to a saddle and follow the ridge north-northwest up mild slopes to the next high point. A short descent leads to another saddle, after which you ascend once again, to Peak 9422 (as shown of the *Caples Lake* topo map), 3.25 miles from the trailhead.

A half-mile descent brings you to the start of the final, lengthy ascent along the ridge to Little Round Top. Initially, the route climbs over moderate slopes to Point 9325, after which the terrain mellows considerably as the ridge sweeps around to the west. For the next 0.75 mile the grade is easy, and then a short moderate climb leads to the summit of Little Round Top.

Even more spectacular views greet you at the summit of Little Round Top. The unobstructed vista covers a vast area of the northern Sierra Nevada, from Lake Tahoe and the surrounding peaks to the north, all the way south to the peaks around Sonora Pass. The more immediate topography is

On the way to Little Round Top Peak

both dramatic and striking in its majesty, particularly the airy summits of both Desolation and Mokelumne Wilderness areas. The trip back to the Sno-Park promises another 5 miles of great views.

FYI: Almost the entire route is near or above 9000 feet, and along a treeless, exposed ridge where high winds are common. Go on a day when the winds are forecast to be light. Along the ridge, avoid the east edge, where enormous cornices appear.

Warm-ups: Rustic Kirkwood Inn boasts of being one of the first resorts to operate in the northern Sierra. Modern-day travelers can partake of freshly cooked dishes created with a local flair for breakfast, lunch, and dinner. The moderately priced establishment also has a full bar and an appetizer menu. Kirkwood Inn is on Highway 88, 0.4 mile west of Caples Lake.

TRIP 48

Winnemucca & Round Top Lakes

see map on page 162

Duration: Three quarters day to full day
Distance: 6–7.5 miles round trip
Difficulty: Moderate–Extreme
Elevation: 8600/9415; 8600/10,381
Maps: *Carson Pass & Caples Lake* 7.5' quadrangles

Introduction: The Carson Pass region boasts of some of the most inspiring terrain in the greater Lake Tahoe area. A high-elevation start that insures good snow conditions over a lengthy season, easy access from a California Sno-Park, and spectacular mountain scenery all combine to make the area south of Carson Pass a very popular destination for winter recreationists. A ban on snowmobiles provides an additional bonus for the non-motorized set. This fashionable route takes snowshoers to two of the area's prettiest and most accessible lakes, backdropped by the impressive slopes of Round Top and The Sisters.

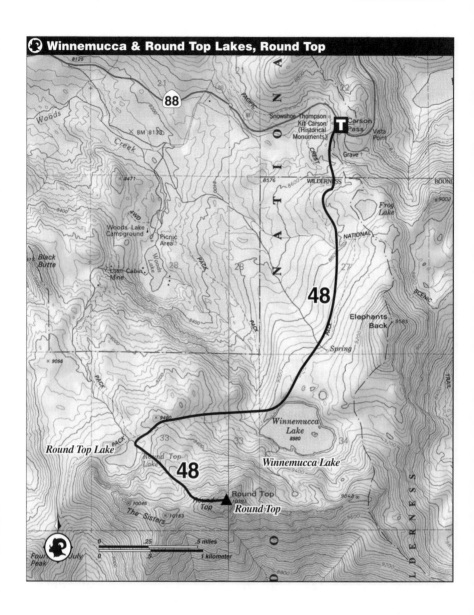

A trip extension to the summit of Round Top provides successful summiteers with one of the most expansive views in the area. The climb is difficult under the best of conditions, which are rarely present. Anyone considering the ascent must be in top physical condition, have the appropriate gear, and be competent alpine climbers.

How to get there: The Carson Pass Sno-Park is on the south side of the highway at Carson Pass, the high point of State Highway 88. You must possess a day permit ($5) or a yearly permit ($25) to legally park at a California Sno-Park. Permits can be purchased Monday through Friday at the Amador Ranger Station, or on weekends at the Carson Pass Information Station.

Description: Head south from the parking area into moderate forest cover, skirting the west side of the ridge that forms this part of the Sierra crest. After 0.25 mile of relatively gentle terrain, you start climbing toward the crest of the ridge through more open forest, reaching the basin that holds Frog Lake at the half-mile point.

From Frog Lake, continue a southerly course on a traverse across the west slopes of Elephants Back through mostly open terrain. Wind-packed snow below Elephants Back may produce less than ideal snow conditions along the traverse, but the conditions should improve as you near the lake. Reach the northwest shore of frozen Winnemucca Lake at 1.8 miles from Carson Pass, where scattered whitebark pines provide a less than adequate windbreak during stiff breezes. The towering north face of 10,381-foot Round Top casts a foreboding shadow over the 8980-foot lake.

Round Top and Winnemucca Lake

Many groups are content with Winnemucca Lake as their destination, but the equally attractive Round Top Lake is just a little over a mile away to the west. The route to Round Top Lake leaves the west shore of Winnemucca Lake to head west up a tributary drainage toward a 9415-foot saddle on a ridge that separates the two lakes' basins. After a nearly mile-long climb you gain the saddle and then make a brief descent to the north shore of Round Top Lake.

The route to the top of Round Top leaves the northeast shore of Round Top Lake and heads southeast up a gully toward the saddle that separates The Sisters from Round Top. Before reaching the saddle, veer left toward a notch in the ridge above and then follow the ridge toward a false summit. Depending on the conditions, you may have to settle for the slightly lower false summit as your goal rather than the true summit, which may require some tricky climbing and a fair bit of exposure to reach.

FYI: Rather than simply retrace your steps from Round Top Lake back to Carson Pass, you could follow a route down Woods Creek to Woods Lake. From there, head north on Woods Lake Road for 0.6 mile to a junction, turn east and follow a road uphill to a meadow 0.1 mile west of Carson Pass.

Snow conditions on Round Top may be less than fantastic, suggesting that parties should consider carrying ice axes and crampons for the ascent.

Warm-ups: Westbound returnees can stop in at rustic Kirkwood Inn, one of the first resorts to operate in the northern Sierra. Modern-day travelers can partake of freshly cooked dishes created with a local flair for breakfast, lunch, and dinner. The moderately priced establishment also has a full bar and an appetizer menu. Kirkwood Inn is on Highway 88, 0.4 mile west of Caples Lake.

Eastbound returnees can dine on fresh-made dishes at Sorensen's Resort, one mile east of the Highway 88–89 junction. The charming café with a quaint mountain setting is open each day from 7:30 A.M. to 9 P.M. serving breakfast, lunch, and dinner. Dinner specialties include beef Burgundy stew, New York steak, and grilled salmon. In between meals patrons can drop by for a cup of hot chocolate, or a glass of beer or wine. In addition to the café, Sorensen's offers comfortable lodging in an assortment of mountain cabins. Call (800) 423-9949 to make a reservation. Check out their lodging packages at **www.sorensensresort.com**.

TRIP **49**

Emigrant Lake

Duration: Three-quarters day
Distance: 8.25 miles round trip
Difficulty: Moderate
Elevation: 7685/8600
Map: *Caples Lake 7.5'* quadrangle

see map
on page
166

Introduction: Two lakes, one huge and easily accessible and one much smaller and harder to reach, provide the dramatic contrasts of this trip. For 2 miles near the beginning of the route, you snowshoe the easy terrain around the south shore of Caples Lake, enjoying the lovely scenery across the immense body of water along the way. At the end of the journey, alpine Emigrant Lake lacks the size of its larger neighbor but possesses a stark beauty nestled in a cirque basin at the base of steep cliffs.

The first 2.5 miles require little in the way of navigation as the path around Caples Lake is clearly defined. Beginners may elect not to proceed any farther than where Emigrant Creek enters the lake at the south end. Beyond Caples Lake, the route passes through thick forest, and finding the entrance to the cirque basin requires a bit more routefinding skill.

Potentially, the trip to Emigrant Lake, which is almost entirely within Mokelumne Wilderness, should provide reasonable solitude. However, some skiers do reach the area around the lake from Kirkwood Meadows via the ski lift in Emigrant Valley.

How to get there: Parking is the chief problem. If you can find a plowed space along Highway 88 close to the Caples Lake dam, grab it. Otherwise, on California State Highway 88, drive to the Kirkwood Cross Country Ski Center parking lot, 0.4 mile west of the dam at Caples Lake. Kirkwood has allowed use of their parking lot for recreationists who are not using their ski trails. The appropriate thing to do would be to politely ask permission to park there, rather than assuming you have a right to do so.

Description: From the Kirkwood Cross Country Ski Center cross to the south side of Highway 88 and climb steeply up the slope. On a general traverse,

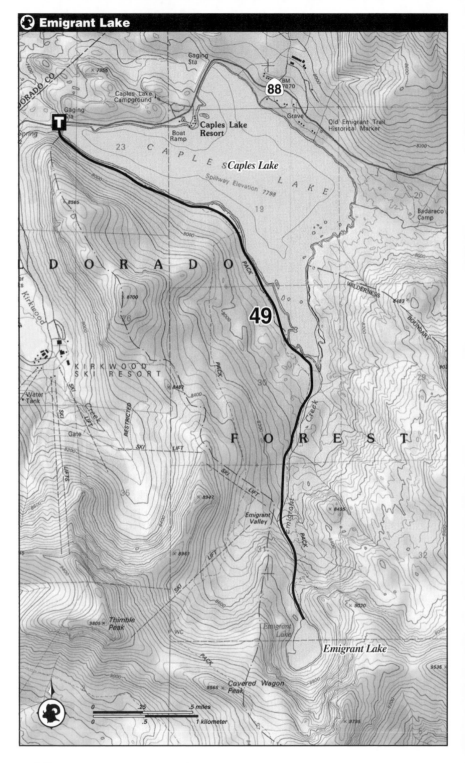

head east toward Caples Lake as you cut across the hillside above the highway. After nearly 0.5 mile, drop to the shoreline of Caples Lake and follow the lake's south edge, paralleling the Mokelumne Wilderness boundary. As you follow the easy terrain along the shoreline of expansive Caples Lake, you can admire the beautiful scenery across the lake. To the northeast lies the long ridge culminating in Little Round Top (see Trip 47) and directly east stands the dark rock of Black Butte. On the point across the lake is the rustic architecture of the Caples Lake Resort.

Two miles of easy snowshoeing beside Caples Lake bring you to the inflow of Emigrant Creek, at the extreme south tip of the lake. Open terrain at the inlet allows you to take your bearings before you enter moderate forest cover, where the route turns south up the drainage. The lake lies at the base of the rock cliffs below Melissa Coray Peak at the head of the canyon.

Turn south and follow the west bank of the creek into a mixed forest of pine and fir. For the next 1.5 miles, you climb mildly through the trees heading upstream along the drainage of Emigrant Creek. Half way up the canyon stay to the left of a prominent rock hill, continuing on a southerly bearing toward the head of the canyon. Routefinding can be a little tricky as you progress up the forested drainage, for Melissa Coray Peak is out of view. Head for the cirque basin immediately east of Covered Wagon Peak, which remains visible at various points along the ascent. About 0.5 mile from the lake the terrain becomes steeper for a short distance before leveling out and then dropping to the shoreline of Emigrant Lake.

The lake is dramatically located in a classic cirque bowl, rimmed by the sheer cliffs of a rock amphitheater. Covered with snow, the horseshoe basin casts a cold and foreboding presence on the winter visitor. The preponderance of avalanche debris piling up at the base of the rock walls at the head of the canyon should discourage any thoughts of possibly progressing too far beyond the lip of the cirque.

FYI: Ambitious mountaineers can extend their journey by ascending one of the peaks (Melissa Corey, Covered Wagon, or Thimble) along the crest of the ridge for a superb view.

Warm-ups: Rustic Kirkwood Inn boasts of being one of the first resorts to operate in the northern Sierra. Modern-day travelers can partake of freshly cooked dishes created with a local flair for breakfast, lunch, and dinner. The moderately priced establishment also has a full bar and an appetizer menu. Kirkwood Inn is on Highway 88, 0.4 mile west of Caples Lake.

TRIP **50**

Echo Lakes

Duration: One-half to three-quarters day
Distance: 2 to 6.5 miles round trip
Difficulty: Easy
Elevation: 7320/7525
Map: *Echo Lakes* 7.5' quadrangle

see map on page **169**

Introduction: Beginning snowshoers will love this journey, which follows a nearly flat, well-marked road to the wide-open expanse of Lower and Upper Echo lakes. The more experienced will recognize this route as the southern gateway into majestic Desolation Wilderness, providing tantalizing temptations for a long day trip or perhaps a multi-day excursion. The openness of the frozen lakes allows you to tailor the length of your trip to the levels of your skills and conditioning. A round trip of 2 miles will get you to the shore of Lower Echo Lake and back, while the journey to the far end of Upper Echo Lake lengthens the round trip to 6.5 miles. The gentle terrain, the lack of routefinding required and the flexibility of choosing your own trip length are elements that novices and more experienced snowshoers will both surely appreciate.

The scenery is great, with sheer rock cliffs and tall ridges rising steeply from the lakeshore. Talking Mountain rises nearly 1500 feet above Lower Echo Lake and, on the opposite side of the basin, Echo Peak rises to a similar height above Upper Echo Lake.

The ease of approach, coupled with the beautiful surroundings, makes the trip into Echo Lakes a very popular one with winter enthusiasts. If you plan to visit the area on a weekend, expect plenty of company. Fortunately, snowmobiles are allowed along Echo Lakes Road only for government business and for access to private homes.

How to get there: Traveling on U.S. 50, find the signed turnoff for the Echo Lakes Sno-Park 1 mile west of Echo Summit. Follow the narrow, plowed road 0.5 mile to the right-hand entrance to the Sno-Park. Plenty of parking

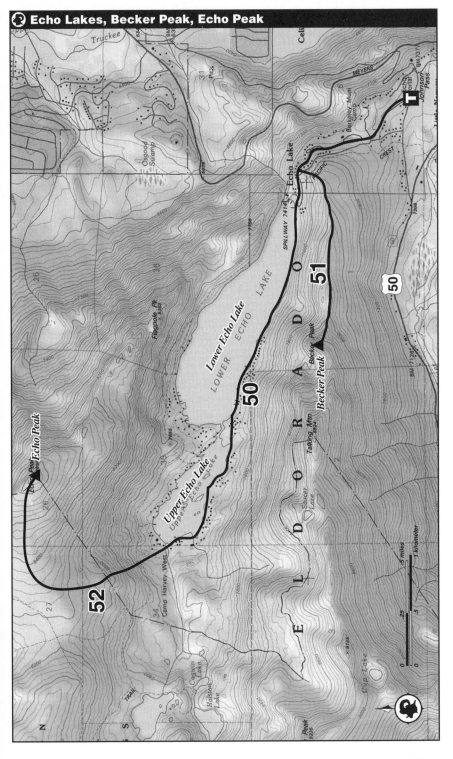

is available as well as a pair of portable toilets. You must possess a day permit ($5) or a yearly permit ($25) to legally park at a California Sno-Park.

Description: Don't look for the beginning of the trail to Echo Lakes within the parking area. Instead, find it opposite the entrance to the Sno-Park and follow the alignment of the Echo Lakes Road as it heads north. More than likely, you will find a packed trail. Many recreationists use this trail, and Cal-Trans will occasionally use it for snow-cats to access the steep slopes northeast of Lower Echo Lake above Highway 50 for avalanche control purposes.

Follow the road for nearly a half mile, until you encounter a junction with a road leading to Berkeley Muni Camp. Bear left at this junction, remaining on the Echo Lakes Road, quickly passing a winter recreation sign with warnings about the possibility of blasting in conjunction with the avalanche-control procedures for Highway 50. As you pass a number of summer cabins, proceed along the course of the road as it makes an almost imperceptible climb toward the lakes. Nearing the first lake, you can abandon the road, which makes a hairpin turn down to the shoreline, and simply head straight down the hillside to the lake, reaching Lower Echo Lake after a mile of easy travel.

Once at the lake, you can tailor your trip to suit your desires. The open, flat terrain is perfectly suited for explorations of varying length. In all but the mildest of winters, the lake freezes deep enough to allow unrestricted travel over the surface, despite warnings to the contrary (no doubt posted purely for liability concerns). However, snowshoe on the lakes with caution, at your own risk, and avoid the areas near the inlet and the outlet, as they tend to thaw before the rest of the lake. Stay off both Upper and Lower Echo Lake when spring temperatures begin to rise.

Please respect the private property in the area by traveling away from the summer homes and cabins surrounding the lakes. Otherwise, enjoy the area at your own pace, traveling as near or as far as you choose.

FYI: If you extend your trip into Desolation Wilderness, even if only for the day, you must obtain a visitor's permit from the Lake Tahoe Basin Management Unit.

Warm-ups: In the shadow of Lover's Leap, historic Strawberry Lodge has been catering to travelers since 1858. The wood-paneled dining room is a fine setting for enjoying good, hearty food at any meal of the day. The dinner menu changes daily, offering diners the freshest cuisine. In winter the restaurant is open Friday through Monday. Strawberry Lodge also has numerous guest rooms and a streamside cabin for overnight stays. Find the lodge on Highway 50, approximately 9 miles east of Kyburz and 9 miles west of Echo Summit. Call (530) 659-7200 for further information, or visit their website at **www.strawberry-lodge.com**.

TRIP **51**

Becker Peak

see map on page 169

Duration: One-half day
Distance: 3.25 miles round trip
Difficulty: Moderate
Elevation: 7320/8325
Map: *Echo Lake* 7.5' quadrangle

Introduction: A reasonably short trip without a tremendous amount of elevation gain leads to a supreme view of the South Lake Tahoe region. You certainly won't be alone for the first part of the trip, as the route follows the extremely popular course to Echo Lakes. However, once you leave the road and head for the summit, the masses are left behind. Routefinding is not particularly difficult (find the ridge and follow it to the top) and only the last slopes below the summit require any extra skill to negotiate. The ascent of Becker Peak is definitely a trip where great rewards require relatively little effort.

How to get there: Traveling on U.S. 50, find the signed turnoff for the Echo Lakes Sno-Park 1 mile west of Echo Summit. Follow the narrow, plowed road 0.5 mile to the right-hand entrance to the Sno-Park. Plenty of parking is available as well as a pair of portable toilets. You must possess a day permit ($5) or a yearly permit ($25) to legally park at a California Sno-Park.

Description: Don't look for the beginning of the trail to Echo Lakes within the parking area. Instead, find it opposite the entrance to the Sno-Park and follow the alignment of the Echo Lakes Road as it heads north. More than likely, you will find a packed trail. Many recreationists use this trail, and Cal-Trans will occasionally use it for snow-cats to access the steep slopes northeast of Lower Echo Lake above Highway 50 for avalanche control purposes.

Follow the road for nearly a half mile, until you encounter a junction with a road leading to Berkeley Muni Camp. Bear left at this junction, remaining on the Echo Lakes Road, quickly passing a winter recreation sign with warnings about the possibility of blasting in conjunction with the avalanche-control procedures for Highway 50. As you pass a number of summer cabins, proceed along the course of the road as it makes an almost imperceptible climb toward the lakes.

Instead of going all the way to Lower Echo Lake, reach the high point on the Echo Lakes Road, 0.85 mile from the trailhead. Leave the road after a curve where both Lake Tahoe and Becker Peak come into view. As you begin a moderately steep climb up the lightly forested hillside, you may notice a couple of old wooden signs, originally painted orange, reading ECHO RIM. Quickly you gain the top of the ridge, where the grade eases and you have limited views of Lake Tahoe in the distance and Lower Echo Lake in the foreground.

The mild ascent along the ridge crest continues for a mile of pleasant snowshoeing through a light covering of fir and pine. Toward the end of the ridge, just before the peak itself, is a small pinnacle that should be passed on the left across a high-angled hillside. Beyond this minor obstacle, you reach the final, steep slopes below the summit of Becker Peak.

The last 150 feet of the ascent are the most difficult part of the trip. The steep angle of the climb combined with less than ideal snow conditions may make the last stretch a bit tricky. The top of the peak is covered by a conglomeration of large rocks that seem to shed most of the snow that falls, producing some tricky footing when a thin covering of snow blankets the

Echo Lake from Becker Peak

summit area. You may elect to pick your way around the rocks or simply drop your snowshoes for the last part of the climb.

However you arrive at the summit the view is sublime. The Echo Lakes area dominates the foreground as the southern gateway to Desolation Wilderness. The incredible vista includes the southern part of Lake Tahoe and the Freel Peak group to the east.

FYI: You can extend your trip by following the ridge another half mile to an even better view atop Talking Mountain. The ascent, although steeper than the trip to Becker Peak, is straightforward and not particularly difficult, with a couple of exceptions. First, you must avoid the cornices along the north side of the ridge. Second, around the midpoint of the climb from Becker Peak, you must pass a large rock outcropping. This area of rock presents the same problem as the summit of Becker Peak: the slick rock typically has a thin covering of snow, making for less than ideal purchase for your snowshoes. In addition, a preponderance of brush covers the hillsides between the rocks, which may also make the slopes hard to negotiate. Combine these elements with a certain amount of exposure down the steep slopes to the south, and this extension can be recommended only for experienced mountain travelers.

Warm-ups: In the shadow of Lover's Leap, historic Strawberry Lodge has been catering to travelers since 1858. The wood-paneled dining room is a good setting for enjoying good, hearty food at any meal of the day. The dinner menu changes daily, offering diners the freshest cuisine. In winter the restaurant is open Friday through Monday. Strawberry Lodge also has numerous guest rooms and a streamside cabin for overnight stays. Find the lodge on Highway 50, approximately 9 miles east of Kyburz and 9 miles west of Echo Summit. Call (530) 659-7200 for further information, or visit their website at **www.strawberry-lodge.com.**

Echo Peak

Duration: Full day
Distance: 9.25 miles
Difficulty: Moderate
Elevation: 7320/8895
Map: *Echo Lakes* 7.5' quadrangle

see map
on page
169

Introduction: A supreme view is the primary attraction of the climb to Echo Peak. Except for the last mile, most of the route is over gentle terrain, with nearly insignificant elevation change. The last mile is moderately steep, but not particularly taxing by snowshoe standards. The climb is fairly popular with backcountry skiers—especially for the descent.

How to get there: Traveling on U.S. 50, find the signed turnoff for the Echo Lakes Sno-Park 1 mile west of Echo Summit. Follow the narrow, plowed road 0.5 mile to the right-hand entrance to the Sno-Park. Plenty of parking is available as well as a pair of portable toilets. You must possess a day permit ($5) or a yearly permit ($25) to legally park at a California Sno-Park.

Description: Don't look for the beginning of the trail to Echo Lakes within the parking area. Instead, find it opposite the entrance to the Sno-Park and follow the alignment of the Echo Lakes Road as it heads north. More than likely, you will find a packed trail. Many recreationists use this trail, and Caltrans will occasionally use it for snow-cats to access the steep slopes northeast of Lower Echo Lake above Highway 50 for avalanche control purposes.

Follow the road for nearly a half mile, until you encounter a junction with a road leading to Berkeley Muni Camp. Bear left at this junction, remaining on the Echo Lakes Road, quickly passing a winter recreation sign with warnings about the possibility of blasting in conjunction with the avalanche-control procedures for Highway 50. As you pass a number of summer cabins, proceed along the course of the road as it makes an almost imperceptible climb toward the lakes. Nearing the first lake, you can abandon the road, which makes a hairpin turn down to the shoreline, and simply head straight down the hillside to the lake, reaching Lower Echo Lake after a mile of easy travel. The open, flat terrain of the lakes is well suited for winter travel. In all but the mildest of winters, the lakes freeze deep enough to allow unrestricted travel over the surface, despite warnings to the contrary (no doubt posted purely for liability concerns). However, snowshoe on the lakes with caution, at your own risk, and avoid the areas near the inlet and the outlet, as they tend to thaw before the rest of the lake. Stay off both Upper and Lower Echo Lake when spring temperatures begin to rise.

From the upper lake, begin ascending moderately steep slopes on a northwest and then northeast bearing through a light covering of mixed forest. The trees begin to thin as you near the summit, allowing for fine views of the Echo Lakes region. After a mile of climbing and 1500 feet of elevation gain, you reach the summit of Echo Peak.

The view from the top is quite impressive, a completely unobstructed vista. Angora Lakes lie at your feet, and beyond are both Fallen Leaf Lake and Lake Tahoe. To the west is an extraordinary view of the Crystal Range peaks. To the south and more distant, the peaks of the Carson Pass area include Red Lake Peak, Stevens Peak and Round Top.

FYI: Check with the Forest Service regarding avalanche conditions before going on this trip. Both the slopes above the lakes and on those on Echo Peak itself are potentially hazardous.

Warm-ups: In the shadow of Lover's Leap, historic Strawberry Lodge has been catering to travelers since 1858. The wood-paneled dining room is a good setting for enjoying good, hearty food at any meal of the day. The dinner menu changes daily, offering diners the freshest cuisine. In winter the restaurant is open Friday through Monday. Strawberry Lodge also has numerous guest rooms and a streamside cabin for overnight stays. Find the lodge on Highway 50, approximately 9 miles east of Kyburz and 9 miles west of Echo Summit. Call (530) 659-7200 for further information, or visit their website at **www.strawberry-lodge.com**.

TRIP **53**

Ralston Peak

Duration: Three-quarter day
Distance: 5 miles round trip
Difficulty: Difficult
Elevation: 6530/9235
Map: *Echo Lake* 7.5' quadrangle

see map
on page
177

Introduction: If you can successfully solve the parking problem and gain access to the trailhead, this trip to the summit of Ralston Peak will bless you with incredible views in all directions. Along the way, the view of Pyramid Creek canyon from the ridge crest is extremely impressive as well. The 2.5-mile climb is moderately steep, gaining 2700 feet on an almost continuous ascent, but should present few problems to snowshoers of intermediate skills. Due to the parking problem, you can be nearly assured of having the superb vistas all to yourself.

How to get there: Finding a place to park will be the most difficult obstacle of the entire trip. Along U.S. 50, 4.8 miles west from Echo Summit, find a small plowed area barely large enough for 4 or 5 cars. This space is near Camp Sacramento, at the beginning of a paved access road.

Description: Cross Highway 50 and begin climbing up the hillside above the westbound lanes. Pass through a moderate cover of mixed forest, heading for the ridge east of the precipitous canyon of Pyramid Creek. Once at the ridge, you have excellent views down the steep canyon and up toward dramatic Horsetail Falls spilling down the nearly vertical headwall. Farther up the ridge, the views improve as Pyramid Peak and Mt. Price make an appearance above the deep gorge of the creek.

Continue to ascend along the ridge, dropping down from the crest occasionally to pass around some steeper projections. Ralston Peak is not an impressive-looking mountain, lacking the alpine flair of its neighbors across the canyon to the west. However, the view *from* the top more than compensates for the view *of* the top.

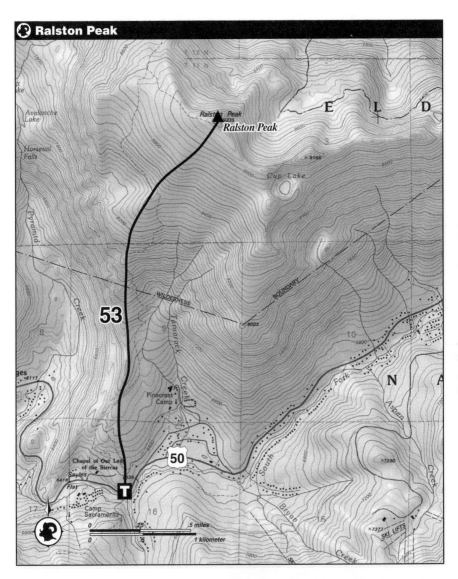

Ralston Peak

About 1.75 mile into the trip, bend northeast and head directly for the summit of Ralston Peak. The trees begin to thin as you gain elevation—ultimately the only trees remaining are some weather-beaten, twisted whitebark pines. Reach the broad summit 2.5 miles from Highway 50.

As promised, the view from the summit is magnificent. Pyramid Peak and Desolation Wilderness dominate the scenery immediately to the west. Directly below the summit are Ralston, Cagwin, and Tamarack lakes, and just east, the much larger Echo Lakes. On the horizon above Echo Lakes and across Lake Tahoe is Freel Peak, highest mountain in the Tahoe basin, flanked by its slightly lower neighbors, Jobs Peak and Jobs Sister. Lake Tahoe appears in its entire splendor between Mt. Tallac and Echo Peak. To the south you can see Lovers Leap below, and farther out, the peaks around Carson Pass, as well as the runs of the Kirkwood ski area.

FYI: An early start, an ample supply of energy, and arrangements for a car shuttle would enable you to create an exciting 9.5-mile loop trip. From the summit of Ralston Peak, head north to Haypress Meadows and then follow the route of the PCT/Tahoe–Yosemite Trail past Echo Lakes (see Trip 50) and on to the Echo Lakes Sno-Park.

Warm-ups: In the shadow of Lover's Leap, historic Strawberry Lodge has been catering to travelers since 1858. The wood-paneled dining room is a good setting for enjoying good, hearty food at any meal of the day. The dinner menu changes daily, offering diners the freshest cuisine. In winter the

restaurant is open Friday through Monday. Strawberry Lodge also has numerous guest rooms and a streamside cabin for overnight stays. Find the lodge on Highway 50, approximately 9 miles east of Kyburz and 9 miles west of Echo Summit. Call (530) 659-7200 for further information, or visit their website at **www.strawberry-lodge .com**.

Tree on Ralston Peak

TRIP 54

Angora Lookout & Angora Lakes

see map on page **181**

Duration: One-half day
Distance: 3.75 miles round trip to Angora Lookout
6.75 miles round trip to Angora Lakes
Difficulty: Easy to Angora Lookout
Moderate to Angora Lakes
Elevation: 6670/7285
6670/7450
Maps: *Emerald Bay & Echo Lakes* 7.5' quadrangles

Introduction: Throngs of summer visitors to Fallen Leaf Lake are permitted to drive their vehicles all the way to Angora Lookout for a superb view, and most of the distance to Angora Lakes for an afternoon of fishing, boating, or sunbathing. Although snowmobilers are afforded the same freedom of access, the lookout and the lakes have far fewer visitors in winter. But, the view from the lookout is still exceptional and the lakes are much more peaceful when snow blankets the ground.

The route to Angora Lookout follows an unbending road all the way to the summit, requiring little in the way of navigational ability. The route beyond the lookout to Angora Lakes is straightforward as well, but does necessitate a bit more routefinding skill. The lakes and the lookout received their name from a herd of Angora goats that were once pastured in the area by Nathan Gilmore.

How to get there: From the Y in South Lake Tahoe, at the junction of Highways 50 and 89, head west on Lake Tahoe Boulevard 2.4 miles to Tahoe Mountain Road. Turn right onto Tahoe Mountain Road, climb another mile to Glenmore Way, and turn right. Immediately, turn left onto Dundee Circle and proceed until you reach Tahoe Mountain Road again. Park near this intersection as space allows. Do not proceed any farther down Tahoe

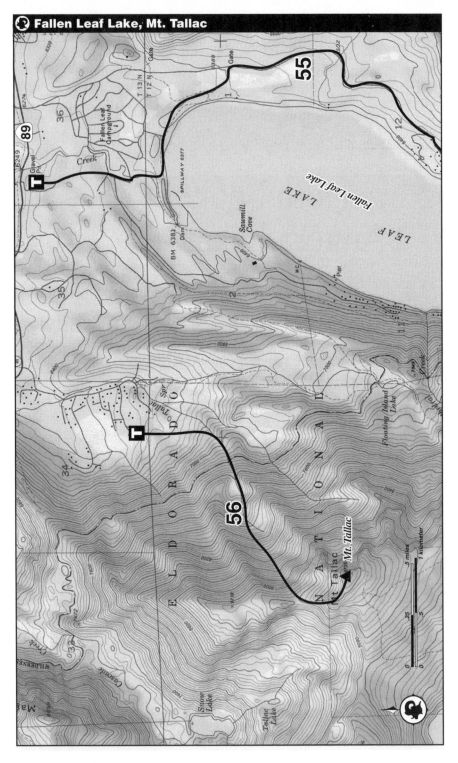

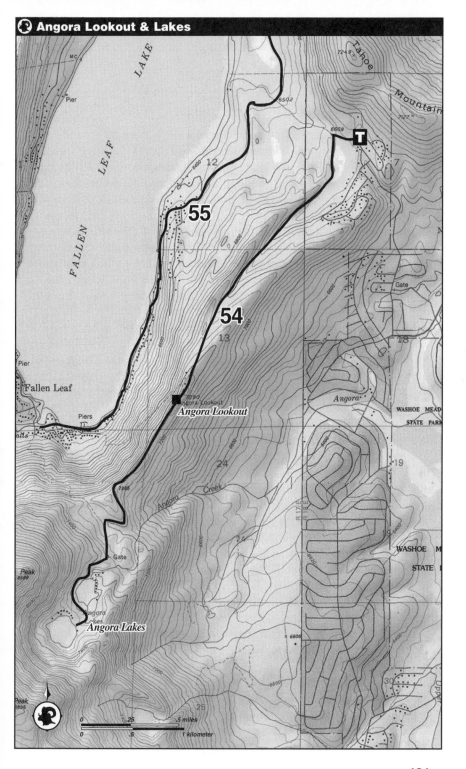

Mountain Road toward Fallen Leaf Lake, even if the road has been plowed, as there is no place to park.

Description: From the parking area, descend along the road 0.1 mile until you reach the beginning of Forest Service Road 12N14. Turn left, heading south on the snow-covered road, passing a meadow lined by quaking aspens. Beyond the meadow, continue straight ahead, following the course of the road on a very mellow grade through a mixed forest of pine, fir, and cedar.

After the first half mile, the road begins to climb as the terrain becomes gradually steeper. A steady ascent eventually brings the route near the crest of the ridge, where incomplete views tantalize the visitor with expectations of a better vista to come. Nearing the summit, telephone wires crossing above the road reveal the location of the lookout, nearly 2 miles from the trailhead.

The view from Angora Lookout is remarkable. Fallen Leaf Lake is directly below, seemingly a stone's throw away. The impressive east face of Mt. Tallac appears across the azure waters of the lake. Dominating the landscape to the north, a piece of Lake Tahoe glistens in the low-angled rays of the winter sun. The snowy summit of Ralston Peak dominates a ridge of peaks guarding the southern boundary of Desolation Wilderness. The commanding presence of Freel Peak, highest summit in the Tahoe basin, appears in the distance to the southeast.

From the lookout, another 1.5 miles of snowshoeing bring you to the matching set of frozen gems known as Angora Lakes. Continue southwest along the road from the lookout as it follows the slight decline of the ridge crest. At the base of a rise, the road quickly bends left to circumvent the hill ahead. You can shave off a bit of time by leaving the road and climbing directly over the hill, regaining the road on the far side. Otherwise, follow the road on a mild descent as it angles around the hill.

On the far side of the hill, the road bends south and begins a moderately steep climb up to the first Angora Lake. Thankfully, snowmobiles are banned beyond this point. If you have trouble determining the exact location of the road, follow the power lines that run up the hill to the summer homes along the north and east shores of Lower Angora Lake. As you near the lake, the terrain flattens allowing you to gently ascend the last 100 yards to the shore.

Angora Lakes nestle in their basins at the bottoms of steep cliffs that form the east face of 8588-foot Angora Peak. To reach Upper Angora Lake, head for the low notch through which a stream connects the upper and lower lakes in summer. Many private cabins ring the shorelines of both lakes—please be respectful of the private property.

FYI: The lookout is an excellent place from which to observe the geological features of the region, including numerous moraines left by retreating glaciers, as well as a couple of cirque basins.

Warm-ups: Mexican food is a sure-fire way to heat up after a day in the winter snow. The Cantina Bar & Grill, which opened in 1977 and is located on Highway 89 just north of the Y in South Lake Tahoe, will spice up your palate with a variety of Mexican and Southwest dishes. The restaurant has regularly received "Best Mexican Restaurant" and "Best Tahoe Margarita" awards. Phone (530) 544-1233 for details, or see a menu at **www.cantinatahoe.com.**

TRIP 55

Fallen Leaf Lake

Duration: One-half to full day
Distance: 3 to 11 miles round trip
Difficulty: Easy
Elevation: 6300/6550
Map: *Emerald Bay* 7.5' quadrangle

see maps
on pages
180, 181

Introduction: The easy terrain around Fallen Leaf Lake, lacking any significant elevation change, is ideally suited for beginning snowshoers and cross-country skiers alike. The area is quite popular on weekends during periods of nice weather, when hundreds of skiers kick and glide on one of four marked trails around the north end of the lake. If you follow one of these established trails, stay off the ski tracks. In addition to human-powered recreationists, snowmobiles are permitted to use the land south of Highway 89 also. Be prepared to share this area with the weekend hordes.

When planning your visit, you can create a trip of whatever length suits your schedule and physical condition. The minimum distance from the Sno-Park to the lake is 1.5 miles, while a trip to the far shore and back will cover 11 miles. Whichever route you choose, once you reach the shore you have wonderful views across the lake to the rugged east faces of Mt. Tallac and Cathedral Peak. Although it is possible to make a complete circumnavigation of the lake, the west side is steep and prone to avalanches.

How to get there: From the Y in South Lake Tahoe, drive north on Highway 89, 3.3 miles to the turnoff for the Taylor Creek Sno-Park. This junction is approximately 1 mile north of Camp Richardson. Turn south into the Sno-Park and park as conditions allow.

Description: There are a variety of cross-country trails around the north end of Fallen Leaf Lake, emanating from the Taylor Creek Sno-Park. You can follow one of these trails, or make your own path to the lake. Taking the most direct path to the lake will still require 0.75 mile of snowshoeing.

If you want to spend the day traveling to the south shore and back, follow a path east through the Fallen Leaf Campground to Fallen Leaf Road. Head south along the road, passing a large meadow to your right. Eventually the road heads toward Fallen Leaf Lake, where you have nice views across the lake of Mt. Tallac and Cathedral Peak. Continue around the east shore to the south end of the lake.

FYI: Extending your trip to Angora Lookout or Angora Lakes is possible by ascending Tahoe Mountain Road 0.4 mile from Fallen Leaf Road to Forest Service Road 12N14. From there follow the description in Trip 54.

Warm-ups: The Beacon Restaurant, overlooking the shore of the lake near Camp Richardson at 1900 Jameson Beach Road, is a favorite haunt of both locals and tourists for lunch and dinner daily, and for weekend brunch. Tantalizing dinner entrees include macadamia salmon and the Crab Feast. Reservations are recommended on weekends ((530) 541-0630).

TRIP **56**

Mt. Tallac

see map
on page
180

Duration: Full day
Distance: 4.5 miles round trip
Difficulty: Extreme
Elevation: 6530/9735
Map: *Emerald Bay* 7.5' quadrangle

Introduction: Many consider Mt. Tallac to be the quintessential Tahoe peak and a successful journey to the summit the area's premier achievement. Certainly, the peak itself dominates the landscape majestically at the south end of the lake, its black hulk showing a rugged pose from almost every vantage point. The peak rises almost 3500 feet from lake level in a mere 3 air miles, forming a spectacular profile for visitors and residents alike. Even the casino crowd has a hard time ignoring the stature of Mt. Tallac. The name "Tallac" comes from a Washoe Indian word meaning "great mountain"—in this case, certainly an accurate appellation.

The ascent, although not long, is demanding both technically and physically. Gaining 3200 feet in a mere 2.25 miles marks this as definitely a trip only for the very experienced and well conditioned. The ascent and descent are both extremely steep for almost the entire distance, requiring that snowshoers be completely comfortable with high-angle slopes.

In addition to the physical and technical demands, the climb should be undertaken only when snow conditions are stable, as the avalanches on Tallac are notorious (see FYI below). Due to the avalanche potential, most attempts are made in late winter or early spring when the snow is typically more consolidated than earlier in the season. A spring ascent invariably will pass at least some evidence of the previous winter's slides.

Accomplished skiers and snowboarders will thrill to the possibilities of a descent from Mt. Tallac. The downhill ride is quite popular with the backcountry crowd, and chances are you will see a number of parties cavorting down the slopes on a sunny weekend. Perhaps as many climb the peak for the trip down as for the ascent, or for the spectacular views.

View from summit of Mt. Tallac

How to get there: Travel northbound on Highway 89, 4.3 miles from the junction with U.S. Highway 50 at the Y in South Lake Tahoe, to the signed turnoff for Spring Creek Road. On Spring Creek Road go 0.6 mile to Pomo Road, and turn right. Follow Pomo Road, signed as Forest Road 1396, another 0.3 mile to its end where there is limited parking along the roadside.

Description: From the end of the road, break out of the trees and head toward the open gully immediately above you (the standard ski route heads farther south before turning southwest up easier slopes). Ascend directly up the steep gully, pausing periodically to admire the beautiful views of Lake Tahoe. After 1000 vertical feet of climbing, the grade abates momentarily as you enter a bowl, where you may see some avalanche debris.

The steep ascent resumes beyond the edge of the bowl. Veering slightly left (southwest), continue the steep climb through widely scattered trees, arcing toward the Mt. Tallac's north ridge above. Another 1800 vertical feet brings you to the crest of the north ridge, a mere 1.5 miles from the trailhead but 2800 feet higher. Here the grade eases considerably—at least for the moment. From the ridge you have a dramatic view of the last slopes below the summit, as well as a spectacular vista of the surrounding topography.

Turn south and follow the ridge as it dips to a saddle. From the saddle, you have a couple of options for the final ascent, depending on the snow conditions and your level of comfort. The easier option, and the preferable one when snow conditions on the face are hard, is to work your way up and around the ridge and then climb to the summit from the back side of the peak. A more direct, but steeper, route is to make an angling ascent across the north face of Mt. Tallac and then climb steeply up the final slopes to the top.

Avalanche run on Mt. Tallac

The view from the summit is unparalleled in the Tahoe Basin. Nearly 3500 feet immediately below, Lake Tahoe is the preeminent gem, seen almost in its entirety. Across the lake to the east is Mt. Rose, third highest peak in the Tahoe basin, and farther south are Freel Peak and Jobs Sister, numbers one and two respectively. The rugged topography directly adjacent to Mt. Tallac comprises perhaps the most impressive scenery. The peaks, lakes, and canyons of Desolation Wilderness create a visual masterpiece, breathtaking to behold. If conditions at the summit are favorable, hours can pass by nearly unnoticed as you admire nature's handiwork.

FYI: For a trip with not as much avalanche potential and less precipitous slopes, you can accept the slightly easier challenge of the north ridge route. This trip begins 0.4 mile up Mattole Road from Spring Creek Road. Climb northwest, directly up the hillside, and gain the north ridge. Turning southwest, follow the ridge until you reach a point on the crest of the north ridge where this route converges with the description above. Although somewhat safer than the direct path, there still is avalanche potential along this route, particularly just below the summit.

Warm-ups: Mexican food is a sure-fire way to heat up after a day in the winter snow. The Cantina Bar & Grill, which opened in 1977 and is located on Highway 89 just north of the Y in South Lake Tahoe, will spice up your palate with a variety of Mexican and Southwest dishes. The restaurant has regularly received "Best Mexican Restaurant" and "Best Tahoe Margarita" awards. Phone (530) 544-1233 for details, or see a menu at **www.cantinatahoe.com**.

CHAPTER 8

WEST TAHOE

In this guide, west Tahoe covers an area roughly from Tahoe City south to Meeks Bay. Aside from the Highway 89 corridor, the west side is perhaps the most serene and peaceful shore of the lake, characterized by deep forests and trickling streams. A number of pleasant trips proceed alongside creeks lined with tall conifers, and many reach pristine lakes and scenic meadows.

Most of these routes begin at an elevation near lake level, typically limiting their season to the true months of winter. Stanford Rock, at 8473 feet, is the only destination on the west side that even approaches a significantly high elevation. Hence, snow conditions can run the gamut from dry powder left over from Pacific cold fronts to wet spring-like mush. Thankfully, the moderate forest cover shades much of the snowpack, which assists in regulating the condition of the snow over much of the area during the height of winter. Once the warmer temperatures of spring arrive and the snow line begins to creep up the hillsides, the season on this side of the lake quickly ends.

Difficulty ratings for the west-side trips are easy or moderate, allowing plenty of opportunities for beginners and those of moderate skill to explore the riches of the Tahoe backcountry. Aside from Stanford Rock, the majority of trips follow mild grades. Sugar Pine Point State Park and Meeks Creek are two excellent areas where neophytes can get a feel for the art of snowshoeing. In general, all the routes proceed across mild terrain, and require minimal navigational skills.

Many of these routes follow established cross-country ski routes for at least part of the way. West-side trails have long been popular with skiers, and sharing the path with your fellow winter travelers is a foregone conclusion. Remember to observe proper trail etiquette (see Chapter 2) in commonly used areas. The initial segments of trails in Sugar Pine Point State Park and Blackwood Canyon are the two areas where you are most likely to see skiers. Unfortunately, snowmobiles are also allowed in Blackwood Canyon.

Access to trailheads along the west shore is quite good. Except for Meeks Creek and Page Meadows, all the trails described in this section begin at either the Blackwood Canyon Sno-Park or the Sugar Pine Point State Park winter parking area. Both facilities provide plenty of parking and sanitation facilities, but both require a fee also. If you are tempted to try routes starting at other locations, be careful, as Placer County has cracked down on vehicles parked on the shoulder of residential streets and county roads during winter.

Snowshoers on road

T R I P 57

Meeks Creek

Duration: One-half day
Distance: 3.5 miles round trip
Difficulty: Easy
Elevation: 6240/6350
Maps: *Homewood & Meeks Bay* 7.5' quadrangles

see map
on page
192

Introduction: Meeks Creek is a good haven when the weather is less than agreeable at the higher elevations. In addition, the essentially flat terrain is ideal for beginners who want to test out their "snow legs." The smooth valley extends for a mile and a half before steeper topography guards the access into Desolation Wilderness.

How to get there: Go south on Highway 89, 10.4 miles from the junction with California Highway 28 in Tahoe City (or 15.3 miles from the Y in South Lake Tahoe, provided Highway 89 around Emerald Bay is open). Park along the west shoulder of the highway.

Description: Begin your trip near an old wooden structure and a Forest Service signboard. Pass over a gate and proceed southwest following the course of closed Forest Service Road 14N32. Continue up the broad valley, which allows pleasant views of the meadows lining Meeks Creek. Although the established route follows the road, the terrain is open enough to allow you to set your own path up the valley.

At the far end of the meadows, you enter a more substantial stand of trees. The road terminates on top of a short rise, where you have limited views farther up the canyon. This is a good spot for lunch before you head back to the car; a short distance beyond this knoll the terrain becomes much steeper.

FYI: If you can find a safe way across the creek at the far end of the meadows, you can alter your return by snowshoeing on the south side of the creek back to the car.

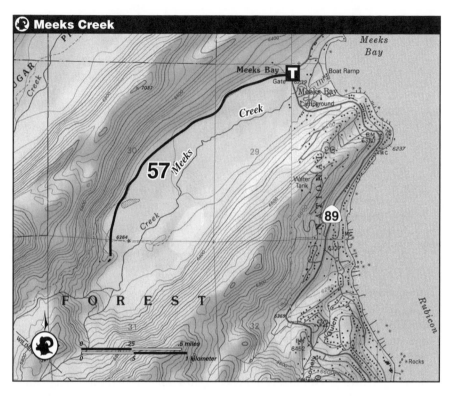

Warm-ups: In the heart of Homewood, the Old Tahoe Cafe dishes up ample portions of hearty meals at a reasonable cost for breakfast and lunch (7 A.M. until 2 P.M.). If you haven't been able to find "real" milkshakes lately, look no further than the Old Tahoe Cafe, located at 5335 W. Lake Blvd.

TRIP 58

Sugar Pine Point State Park

Duration: One-half day
Distance: 2.1 to 3.3 miles
Difficulty: Easy
Elevation: 6320
Maps: *Meeks Bay & Homewood* 7.5' quadrangle

see map
on page
194

Introduction: Snowshoers looking for the combination of pleasant scenery, gentle terrain, and marked trails will find Sugar Pine Point State Park to be an answer to their dreams. The park offers four marked routes that traverse essentially flat terrain, two on serene, forested routes to the west of Highway 89 and two east of the highway that offer lake views and a bit of Tahoe history.

In previous years State Parks used to set cross-country ski tracks along the four marked trails but has for now discontinued this practice. Please observe proper snowshoeing etiquette and refrain from walking in ski tracks when present.

How to get there: From the junction with California Highway 28 in Tahoe City, go south on Highway 89 for about 9 miles to Sugar Pine Point State Park. The park has a north and south entrance. The north entrance leads to the campground and trailhead parking for the Yellow, Blue, and Red ski trails. The south entrance provides parking for the Orange and Yellow ski trails. Both entrances require a $6.00 per day fee for parking.

Description:

YELLOW TRAIL: The 2-mile Yellow Trail can be accessed from either the north or south parking area. The trail passes through the Edward L. Z'berg Natural Preserve, travels along the shore of Lake Tahoe to the Sugar Pine Point Lighthouse and then loops back through the forest to the trailhead.

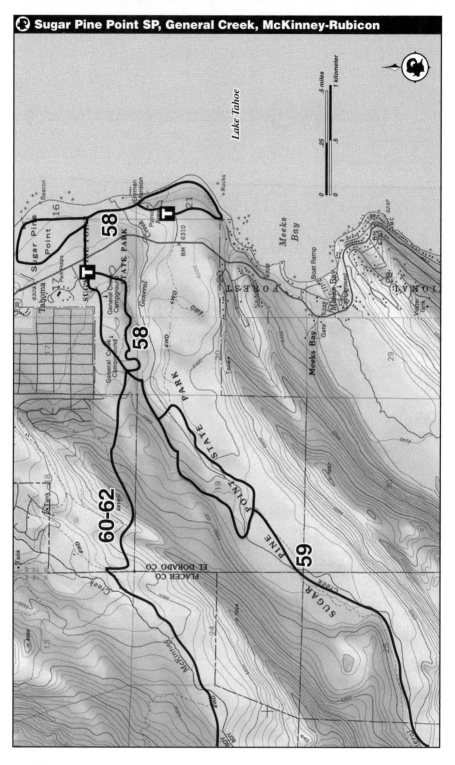

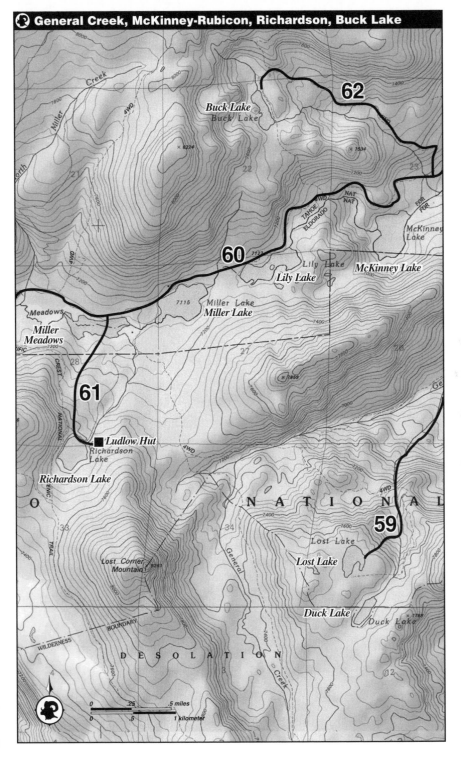

Creek

Miller

North

Buck Lake
Buck Lake

62

× 8224

× 7834

21

22

23

4WD

NAT
NAT

TAHOE
ELDORADO

FOR
FOR

McKinney
Lake

60

7127

Lily Lake
Lily Lake

McKinney Lake

Meadows

7115

Miller Lake
Miller Lake

Miller
Meadows

PACIFIC

CREST

NATIONAL

28

27

× 7859

26

25

61

■ *Ludlow Hut*

Richardson
Lake

4WD

Richardson Lake

SCENIC

TRAIL

O

N A T I O N A L

4WD

59

33

34

Lost Lake

Lost Lake

General

Ge

Lost Corner
Mountain 8261

WILDERNESS

BOUNDARY

D E S O L A T I O N

Duck Lake

Duck Lake
× 7789

Creek

0   .25   .5 miles
0   .5   1 kilometer

ORANGE TRAIL: A counterclockwise journey along this 1.2-mile long loop travels through the forest to the lake, passes by the South Boathouse and continues along the scenic lakeshore to the vicinity of the Hellman-Ehrman Mansion, built in 1903 before returning to the parking area.

BLUE TRAIL: From the parking area, follow the 2.1-mile Blue Trail through medium forest cover, bearing left at the first junction. Maps have been placed at each major junction, making travel through the park quite easy for all skill levels—you would have to be Mr. Magoo to get lost. Soon, you reach a junction of the blue and red trails, where you bear right and follow the Blue Trail as it loops back to the parking area.

RED TRAIL: To complete the 3.3-mile Red Trail you must proceed as described above on the Blue Trail to the second junction. Continue ahead until the route bends left, passes a small meadow, and turns southeast at a junction to cross General Creek on a bridge. As you continue along the south side of the creek, the forest begins to lessen, allowing for limited views. Near Olympic Meadows, site of the 1960 Olympic Shooting Range, you follow the marked trail to a bridge over General Creek and then loop back to the east along the north side of General Creek to the junction. From there retrace your steps back to the parking lot.

FYI: For those who don't mind camping in the snow, Sugar Pine Point State Park's campground, with heated restrooms and showers, is open during the winter, providing a fine base camp for exploring all four of the routes.

Warm-ups: Jake's Lake Tahoe has been serving exquisite seafood cuisine from the northwest shore of Lake Tahoe for over 25 years. The casual atmosphere is a fine complement to the tantalizing dishes from either the lunch or dinner menus. Try the pan-fried crabcakes with meyer lemon remoulade for an appetizer, or the fennel-crusted halibut with chardonnay truffle sauce for a dinner entrée. You can't go wrong with a bowl of the seafood chowder if you're looking for lighter fare. Landlubbers can choose from a fine selection of grilled meats. The restaurant is located at the south end of Tahoe City in the Boatworks Mall at 780 N. Lake Blvd. Call (530) 583-0188 for reservations or visit their website at **www.jakestahoe.com**.

TRIP 59

General Creek

Duration: One-half to full day
Distance: 4.5 to 10 miles
Difficulty: Easy to moderate
Elevation: 6320/7700
Maps: *Meeks Bay & Homewood* 7.5' quadrangles

see maps
on pages
194, 195

Introduction: General Creek offers a more ambitious undertaking than the previous trip on marked trails through Sugar Pine Point State Park. Experienced wilderness travelers can proceed from the campground up the drainage for quite a distance beyond the end of the trail system. Two forested lakes perch 1000 feet above the floor of General Creek and 5 miles from the trailhead, accessible only by a stiff, mile-plus climb. Highly skilled adventurers will find that the trip along General Creek has much to offer.

How to get there: Go south on Highway 89, 8.9 miles from the junction with California Highway 28 in Tahoe City to the well-marked entrance to Sugar Pine Point State Park. Pass the entrance station, where you must pay $6.00 for a parking permit, and proceed to the large parking area, 0.2 mile from the highway (portable toilets are available).

Description: Begin snowshoeing through medium forest cover on the park's marked blue route, bearing left at the first junction. Maps have been placed at each major junction, making travel through the park quite easy for all skill levels—you would have to be Mr. Magoo to get lost. Quickly, you reach a point where the blue and red trails converge. Follow the red trail as it continues a level track up the valley.

The route bends left, passes a small meadow, and then crosses General Creek on a bridge. As you continue along the south side of the creek, the forest begins to lessen, allowing for limited views. Near Olympic Meadows, the trees thin even more, improving the view up the canyon. Follow the red route past the loop connection to the far end, 2.25 miles from the parking lot.

Here you can leave the marked trail behind, and forge ahead into unmarked territory. Proceed up the south bank of General Creek as it cuts through medium forest. After 1.5 miles from the end of the loop, a tributary creek from Lost and Duck lakes joins the main branch of General Creek. Follow this drainage up steeper terrain another 1.25 miles to the frozen lakes.

FYI: The State Park also offers year-round camping for a fee. Hot showers and running water are part of the package, but space is limited in winter.

Warm-ups: Jake's Lake Tahoe has been serving exquisite seafood cuisine from the northwest shore of Lake Tahoe for over 25 years. The casual atmosphere is a fine complement to the tantalizing dishes from either the lunch or dinner menus. Try the pan-fried crabcakes with meyer lemon remoulade for an appetizer, or the fennel-crusted halibut with chardonnay truffle sauce for a dinner entrée. You can't go wrong with a bowl of the seafood chowder if you're looking for lighter fare. Landlubbers can choose from a fine selection of grilled meats. The restaurant is located at the south end of Tahoe City in the Boatworks Mall at 780 N. Lake Blvd. Call (530) 583-0188 for reservations or visit their website at **www.jakestahoe.com.**

General Creek

TRIP 60

McKinney, Lily & Miller Lakes & Miller Meadows

see maps on pages 194, 195

Duration: One-half to three-quarters day
Distance: 7 miles round trip to McKinney Lake
12 miles round trip to Miller Meadows
Difficulty: Moderate
Elevation: 6320/7100
Maps: *Meeks Bay & Homewood* 7.5' quadrangles

Introduction: Most of this route is on a segment of the McKinney–Rubicon OHV road past three fairly large lakes to expansive Miller Meadows. Due to parking restrictions at the beginning of the road (See FYI below), you must begin the trip at Sugar Pine Point State Park and climb over a ridge to access the route. Crossing over the ridge is the most difficult part of the trip, requiring some navigational skills. In the McKinney Creek drainage, the road follows a very mild grade alongside the creek, past the lakes and on to the meadows.

Each of the lakes is a worthy destination in itself, so you can tailor the length of your trip to suit your particular skills and schedules. McKinney, Lily, and Miller lakes all invite further explorations of their shorelines and the surrounding topography. Snowshoeing all the way to the meadows offers a chance for even further investigation amid open and extensive terrain. Pleasant scenery is a nearly constant companion along the full length of this trip.

How to get there: Go south on Highway 89, 8.9 miles from the junction with California Highway 28 in Tahoe City to the well-marked entrance to Sugar Pine Point State Park. Pass the guard house, where you must pay $6.00 for

View of Lake Tahoe McKinney Lake Route

a parking permit, and proceed to the large parking area, 0.2 mile from the highway (portable toilets are available).

Description: Sugar Pine Point State Park has a nice system of marked trails, principally for cross-country ski use. Snowshoers are allowed to use the trails, provided they stay out of the tracks set for the skiers. Begin snowshoeing through medium forest cover on the marked blue route on a very gentle grade, then bear left at the first junction. Quickly, you reach a point where the blue and red trails converge.

From this junction, leave the marked trail and head west, climbing the ridge ahead on a moderate ascent. Your goal is to intersect a road just below Peak 6814 on the *Homewood* topo map, approximately 1.25 mile from the trailhead. Follow this road briefly to the crest of the ridge separating General Creek and McKinney Creek. Continue on the road as it descends toward McKinney Creek, reaching the OHV road 1.9 miles from the Sno-Park.

Back on gentle terrain, follow the road through a light covering of mixed forest, crossing McKinney Creek after a mile and the creek draining Buck Lake in another 0.5 mile.

Climb for a short distance from the second creek crossing, curving around a hillside as the road passes above McKinney Lake, 3.5 miles from the trailhead. McKinney Lake is a relatively large body of water surrounded by forest at the base of a ridge. To visit the lake, you will have to descend the steep hillside to the north shoreline.

From above McKinney Lake, a mild, mile-long climb brings you to Lily Lake, long and narrow, also perched below a ridge and enclosed by trees.

A nearly level half-mile journey now leads to Miller Lake, 5 miles from the trailhead. Tree-lined as well, Miller is a large lake with a pair of forested hills above the opposite shoreline.

From the east edge of Miller Lake, a half-mile of easy travel brings you to the beginning of Miller Meadows, 5.5 miles from the trailhead. Actually a pair of extensive clearings separated by a grove of trees, Miller Meadows provides opportunities for wide-ranging explorations of the meadows and surrounding terrain. Sourdough Hill stands guard over the meadows on the south and provides a good landmark for those wishing to extend their journey to Richardson Lake (see Trip 61).

FYI: Rather than the climb over the ridge from Sugar Pine Point State Park, some reports describe an easier access to the McKinney–Rubicon Road in McKinney Estates subdivision. Unfortunately, county ordinances forbid parking here, even though a plowed area seems perfectly suited for such purposes. Placer County handed out warnings for illegally parked vehicles during previous winters.

Warm-ups: In the heart of Homewood, the Old Tahoe Cafe dishes up ample portions of hearty meals at a reasonable cost for breakfast and lunch (7 A.M. until 2 P.M.). If you haven't been able to find "real" milkshakes lately, look no further than the Old Tahoe Cafe, located at 5335 W. Lake Blvd.

TRIP 61

Richardson Lake & Ludlow Hut

see maps
on pages
194,195

Duration: Full day
Distance: 13.75 miles round trip
Difficulty: Moderate
Elevation: 6320/7445
Maps: *Meeks Bay & Homewood* 7.5' quadrangles

Introduction: Trip 60 to Miller Meadows is packed with beautiful scenery, and this extension to Richardson Lake adds even more. The moderate ascent from the meadows to the lake requires nearly a mile of modest climbing through fairly dense forest, necessitating a certain degree of routefinding. Once at Richardson Lake you can enjoy the serenity of a snow-covered lake with the steep slopes of Sourdough Hill as a backdrop. A night or two at the Sierra Club's Ludlow Hut provides opportunities for even more roaming.

How to get there: Go south on Highway 89, 8.9 miles from the junction with California Highway 28 in Tahoe City to the well-marked entrance to Sugar Pine Point State Park. Pass the guard house, where you must pay $6.00 for a parking permit, and proceed to the large parking area, 0.2 mile from the highway (portable toilets are available).

Description: Sugar Pine Point State Park has a nice system of marked trails, principally for cross-country ski use. Snowshoers are allowed to use the trails, provided they stay out of the tracks set for the skiers. Begin snowshoeing through medium forest cover on the marked blue route on a very gentle grade, then bear left at the first junction. Quickly, you reach a point where the blue and red trails converge.

From this junction, leave the marked trail and head west, climbing the ridge ahead on a moderate ascent. Your goal is to intersect a road just below Peak 6814 on the *Homewood* topo map, approximately 1.25 mile from the trailhead. Follow this road briefly to the crest of the ridge separating General Creek and McKinney Creek. Continue on the road as it descends toward McKinney Creek, reaching the OHV road 1.9 miles from the Sno-Park.

Back on gentle terrain, follow the road through a light covering of mixed forest, crossing McKinney Creek after a mile and the creek draining Buck Lake in another 0.5 mile.

Climb for a short distance from the second creek crossing, curving around a hillside as the road passes above McKinney Lake, 3.5 miles from the trailhead. McKinney Lake is a relatively large body of water surrounded by forest at the base of a ridge. To visit the lake, you will have to descend the steep hillside to the north shoreline.

From above McKinney Lake, a mild, mile-long climb brings you to Lily Lake, long and narrow, also perched below a ridge and enclosed by trees.

A nearly level half-mile journey now leads to Miller Lake, 5 miles from the trailhead. Tree-lined as well, Miller is a large lake with a pair of forested hills above the opposite shoreline.

From the east edge of Miller Lake, a half-mile of easy travel brings you to the beginning of Miller Meadows, 5.5 miles from the trailhead. Approximately 0.5 mile from the beginning of the Meadows, head directly south toward the base of the east slopes of Sourdough Hill. Quickly pass out of the open terrain of the meadows and into moderate forest cover. Continue to make a steady climb through the trees, generally following the route of the Pacific Crest Trail. Reach Richardson Lake 0.75 mile from Miller Meadows and east-southeast of Sourdough Hill's summit.

There are a couple of options for the route to Richardson Lake. You could try to follow the road that leaves Miller Meadows a short distance past the west edge of Miller Lake, but this road is hard to discern. Another alternative is to head up the drainage of the stream that drains the lake. However, with a generous snowpack, this alternate route may also be difficult to follow. Still, locating Richardson Lake is not as difficult as you might think. The lake is in a basin 0.25 mile and 185 feet below the saddle between Sourdough Hill and Lost Corner Mountain, tucked directly into the base of the steep east slopes of Sourdough Hill.

Richardson Lake sits in a picturesque basin beneath lightly forested hillsides. The steep topography of Sourdough Hill and Lost Corner Mountain create a feeling of lonely isolation. This picture of serenity and solitude is an ideal accompaniment for lunch or for a long, relaxing break. Ludlow Hut was built in the mid-Fifties by the Sierra Club, which continues the responsibility for its maintenance. The structure remains in excellent condition despite the easy accessibility to off-road vehicles during the summer months. Find the hut about 100 yards above the east shore.

FYI: For an even greater adventure, rather than backtracking, you could traverse the terrain between Richardson Lake and General Creek, eventually connecting with Trip 59 to create a loop trip back to the Sugar Pine Point State Park parking lot. The distance is virtually the same as returning via the normal route, but you probably would not have the luxury of a packed trail between the lake and the tracks in Sugar Pine Point State Park.

Warm-ups: For use of the Ludlow Hut, make reservations by contacting:

Clair Tappaan Lodge
P.O. Box 36
Norden, CA 95724
(530) 426-3632

TRIP **62**

Buck Lake

Duration: Three-quarter day
Distance: 9.5 miles round trip
Difficulty: Moderate
Elevation: 6320/7550
Maps: *Meeks Bay & Homewood* 7.5' quadrangles

see maps on pages 194, 195

Introduction: A secluded lake off the beaten path is the goal of this trip. You may see other recreationists along the route of the McKinney-Rubicon Road, including snowmobilers, but once you leave the road, most of the machines and people are left behind. The lake itself is quite scenic, a worthy destination set quietly in a long, flat basin enclosed by precipitous cliffs.

How to get there: Go south on Highway 89, 8.9 miles from the junction with California Highway 28 in Tahoe City to the well-marked entrance to Sugar Pine Point State Park. Pass the guard house, where you must pay $6.00 for a parking permit, and proceed to the large parking area, 0.2 mile from the highway (portable toilets are available).

Description: Sugar Pine Point State Park has a nice system of marked trails, principally for cross-country ski use. Snowshoers are allowed to use the trails, provided they stay out of the tracks set for the skiers. Begin snowshoeing through medium forest cover on the marked blue route on a very gentle grade, then bear left at the first junction. Quickly, you reach a point where the blue and red trails converge.

From this junction, leave the marked trail and head west, climbing the ridge ahead on a moderate ascent. Your goal is to intersect a road just below Peak 6814 on the *Homewood* topo map, approximately 1.25 mile from the trailhead. Follow this road briefly to the crest of the ridge separating General Creek and McKinney Creek. Continue on the road as it descends toward McKinney Creek, reaching the OHV road 1.9 miles from the Sno-Park.

Back on gentle terrain, follow the road through a light covering of mixed forest, crossing McKinney Creek after a mile and the creek draining Buck Lake in another 0.5 mile.

Leave the McKinney–Rubicon Road at the creek and turn northwest, following the drainage up a moderately steep hillside. Bear left where the slope of the hillside becomes more moderate to find a 4WD road as it parallels the general course of the drainage. Follow the road in and out of light forest, continuing to gain elevation at a mild rate, until a final climb brings you well above the long valley in which Buck Lake sits. A moderately steep descent from the road delivers you to the lakeshore, 4.75 miles from the trailhead.

Buck Lake occupies a small part of a long, narrow basin rimmed by steep cliffs. In winter the lake itself is almost indistinguishable from the

Buck Lake

smooth valley floor. The pleasant surroundings create a very pleasant lunch spot.

On the return, you briefly have a nice view of Lake Tahoe.

FYI: You can create a nice partial loop trip by continuing to follow the 4WD road from above Buck Lake for 2.75 miles as it curves around to Miller Meadows. Then follow the McKinney–Rubicon Road (see Trip 60) for another 2.75 miles, past Miller, Lily, and McKinney lakes to the point where you left the road to climb to Buck Lake. The total distance is 12 miles.

Warm-ups: In the heart of Homewood, the Old Tahoe Cafe dishes up ample portions of hearty meals at a reasonable cost for breakfast and lunch (7 A.M. until 2 P.M.). If you haven't been able to find "real" milkshakes lately, look no further than the Old Tahoe Cafe, located at 5335 W. Lake Blvd.

T R I P 63

Blackwood Canyon

Duration: One-half to full day
Distance: 4.5 to 14.75 miles round trip
Difficulty: Easy to difficult
Elevation: 6230/7280
Map: *Homewood* 7.5' quadrangle

see maps
on pages
208, 209

Introduction: Blackwood Canyon offers a wide range of experiences for snowshoers of all levels of skill and endurance. The route follows the alignment of the OHV road that motor-powered recreationists use in summertime to travel between Lake Tahoe and the Rubicon River territory. The first 2.25 miles are well suited for an easy half-day journey to the crossing of Blackwood Creek, where you will find the creek coursing sinuously through open meadows—a great lunch spot. For something more challenging, the excursion to Barker Pass offers grand views of the peaks and ridges in the upper canyon. This trip would be rated Easy if not for the total distance of nearly 15 miles round trip. Between these two extremes are moderate trips tailored to your own personal desires. The obvious nature of the road requires almost no routefinding capabilities throughout the entire route.

View of Barker Peak

Aside from the great scenery and the flexibility of choices for possible trips, Blackwood Canyon does have some potential drawbacks. The Sno-Park provides easy access to the area, which is very popular on weekends, particularly when the weather is pleasant. In addition, the road is open to snowmobiles. If you have an aversion to the noisy beasts, visit the canyon on a weekday, or consider Trip 64 to Stanford Rock as an alternative.

How to get there: Go south on Highway 89 for 8.1 miles from its junction with California Highway 28 in Tahoe City to the well-marked entrance for the Blackwood Canyon Sno-Park. Turn west and follow signs a short distance to the large parking lot (portable toilets).

Description: Leave the Sno-Park and follow the wide route of the road as it heads west on an easy grade. The popularity of this area should provide plenty of tracks to follow unless you are the first party after a fresh snowfall. Progressing up the canyon, about 0.5 mile from the trailhead you have a nice view of Twin Peaks up the road cut. Continue up the gentle, almost indiscernible, incline through mixed forest until you reach a bend in the road at 2.25 miles. A lesser road continues straight up the canyon but you should follow the route to the left over Blackwood Creek, pausing to take in the view of the serpentine stream winding across the open floor of the basin.

Beginners and snowshoers looking for a short trip will find the creek a good turnaround point.

On the opposite side of the canyon, the road bends southwest again and begins to climb at a mild rate. Soon you find yourself a good distance above the floor of the canyon. You have gained less than 200 vertical feet in the first 2.5 miles, but beyond the creek the route begins to accumulate elevation at a greater rate, although it is still considered an easy ascent. Better views of the peaks and ridges above Blackwood Canyon come into play as you continue to climb. After gaining 600 feet from the creek crossing, the road crosses the South Fork, 4.6 miles from the trailhead.

The road continues to climb over the next 2.5 miles to Barker Pass, curving around the steep hillsides that form the head of the canyon and crossing the Middle Fork numerous times in the process. Ascending at a more moderate rate, these last miles gain another 800 feet before a 0.25-mile descent leads to the pass. From the pass you have pleasant views of the surrounding peaks and a glimpse of Lake Tahoe. Beyond Barker Pass, the continuation of the OHV road leads to Rubicon River country.

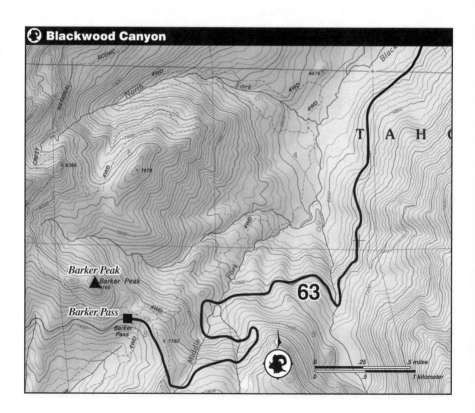

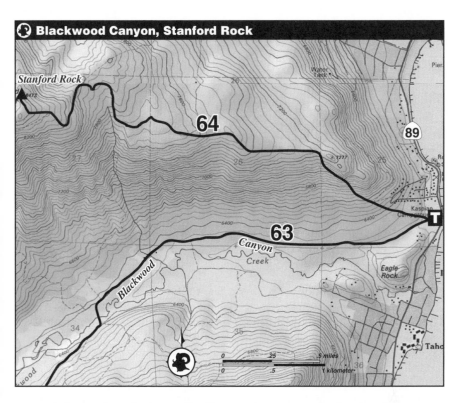

Blackwood Canyon, Stanford Rock

FYI: Advanced parties in search of better views can make the short but steep climb from Barker Pass to the top of Barker Peak. This ascent would add another two-thirds mile and 950 vertical feet, to your already nearly 15-mile round trip.

Warm-ups: Jake's Lake Tahoe has been serving exquisite seafood cuisine from the northwest shore of Lake Tahoe for over 25 years. The casual atmosphere is a fine complement to the tantalizing dishes from either the lunch or dinner menus. Try the pan-fried crabcakes with meyer lemon remoulade for an appetizer, or the fennel-crusted halibut with chardonnay truffle sauce for a dinner entrée. You can't go wrong with a bowl of the seafood chowder if you're looking for lighter fare. Landlubbers can choose from a fine selection of grilled meats. The restaurant is located at the south end of Tahoe City in the Boatworks Mall at 780 N. Lake Blvd. Call (530) 583-0188 for reservations or visit their website at **www.jakestahoe.com**.

Stanford Rock

Duration: Three-quarter day
Distance: 6.5 miles round trip
Difficulty: Moderate
Elevation: 6230/8473
Map: *Homewood* 7.5' quadrangle

see map
on page
209

Introduction: The Blackwood Canyon Sno-Park is heavily used on weekends, but you will leave the crowds behind right from the start of this trip. While the great percentage of those on skis, snowshoes, or snowmobiles journey up Blackwood Canyon, this route to Stanford Rock promises a reasonable amount of solitude. An established cross-country ski route from the north is joined at the halfway point, but is lightly used.

The ascent provides excellent views at various points, and the vista from the summit is quite dramatic. Above the sheer north face of Stanford Rock, Lake Tahoe is seen in its entire splendor, along with the high peaks and ridges above Blackwood Canyon and Ward Creek.

With the exception of gaining the ridge near the beginning, the vast majority of the trip is a moderate ascent and requires only basic routefinding. Most of the route is forested, providing some relief from potentially windy conditions.

How to get there: Go south on Highway 89 for 8.1 miles from its junction with California Highway 28 in Tahoe City to the well-marked entrance for the Blackwood Canyon Sno-Park. Turn west and follow signs a short distance to the large parking lot (portable toilets are available).

Description: Avoiding the well-traveled road, head directly west from the parking lot into dense forest cover. Stay south of the homes in the subdivision to the north and proceed through the trees on a gentle grade approximately one-third mile to a large clearing on the slopes below Peak 7277, shown on the *Homewood* topo map. Assume a steeper course as you begin a curving ascent to the northwest, across the hillside on the way to the ridge above. Beautiful views of Lake Tahoe appear to the rear as you climb across the moderately steep terrain. To the south, Eagle Rock is a nice accent to the emerald waters of the lake. Nearly a mile from the trailhead, in light forest, you reach easier travel along the crest of the ridge, high above Blackwood Canyon.

Follow the ridge on a predominantly mild grade, with a few short slopes of moderate ascent. From a knob 1.5 miles from the trailhead, you have excellent views of Blackwood Canyon, but Lake Tahoe is blocked by trees. Continue to follow the ridge crest another 0.2 mile, until you intersect the snow-covered road used by skiers to reach Stanford Rock from Ward Creek to the north. You can follow the road, which is easy to discern through the moderate forest, or assume a more direct route along the ridge.

If you choose the road option, the route winds across the ridge crest for the next 1.25 miles through moderate forest until reaching a viewpoint nearly 3 miles from the trailhead. From here you have exceptional views of the lake and partial views of Blackwood Canyon. From the viewpoint, turn northwest and make the final quarter-mile climb to the top of Stanford Rock.

View from Stanford Rock

Standing on the wind-blown rocks above the sheer face of Stanford Rock, you can gaze at the majesty of Lake Tahoe, or look north toward the backside of Alpine Meadows, flanked by Scott and Ward peaks. The dramatic form of Twin Peaks guards the upper reaches of Blackwood Canyon at the west end of the ridge.

FYI: The open slope below Peak 7277, beginning one-third mile from the Sno-Park, is covered with boulders and brush. This southern exposure is prone to soft conditions during warm winter periods and in spring, so watch your step, particularly in the afternoons of sunny days. If avalanche conditions are a concern, you may feel safer ascending the ridge in the forested slopes a half-mile farther up the canyon.

Warm-ups: Jake's Lake Tahoe has been serving exquisite seafood cuisine from the northwest shore of Lake Tahoe for over 25 years. The casual atmosphere is a fine complement to the tantalizing dishes from either the lunch or dinner menus. Try the pan-fried crabcakes with meyer lemon remoulade for an appetizer, or the fennel-crusted halibut with chardonnay truffle sauce for a dinner entrée. You can't go wrong with a bowl of the seafood chowder if you're looking for lighter fare. Landlubbers can choose from a fine selection of grilled meats. The restaurant is located at the south end of Tahoe City in the Boatworks Mall at 780 N. Lake Blvd. Call (530) 583-0188 for reservations or visit their website at **www.jakestahoe.com.**

TRIP 65

Page Meadows

see map
on page
213

Duration: One-half day
Distance: 3 miles round trip
Difficulty: Easy
Elevation: 6975/6925
Map: *Tahoe City* 7.5' quadrangle

Introduction: Page Meadows is a handful of clearings strung together to the north of Ward Creek. The nearly level terrain and short distance makes this trip easy enough for snowshoers of all levels. A minimal amount of

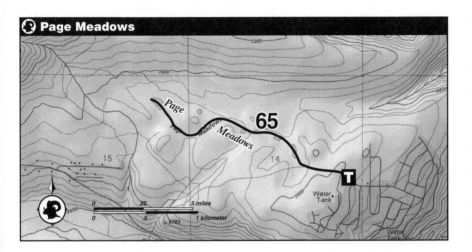

Page Meadows

routefinding is necessary in order to reach the first meadow, but the route is so popular with locals that a beaten trail should usually be present unless it's just after a storm. Once the first meadow is found the remaining meadows are easy to locate. The mostly open meadows provide pleasant scenery, complemented nicely by numerous aspen stands.

How to get there: In the lakeshore community of Sunnyside, about 2 miles south of the junction with Highway 28 in Tahoe City, leave Highway 89 and turn southwest onto Pine Avenue. After 0.2 mile turn right on Tahoe Park Heights and drive 0.7 mile to the top of a hill and a 4-way intersection. Take the middle road, Big Pine, and proceed 0.25 mile to a left-hand turn onto Silvertip Drive. Follow Silvertip to the end of the road and the signed parking area.

Description: Head west from the parking area, following the course of a snow-covered road through mostly fir forest, with lesser amounts of lodgepole and Jeffrey pine. After a slight 0.1-mile climb, the road gently descends for another 0.2 mile to an indistinct point where you leave the road and veer northwest, reaching the first meadow in about 100 yards. From the north end of the first meadow, the route heads generally west-northwest through the other meadows.

FYI: Without a beaten path to guide you, getting off track in the thick forest is a distinct possibility. A GPS unit would be a helpful tool under such circumstances.

Warm-ups: The Fire Sign Café in Tahoe City has been a local hot spot since 1970. The restaurant is extremely busy on weekends but the freshly prepared dishes are worth the wait. Not only will you find breakfast fare like bacon and eggs, but more exotic fare such as the Cape Cod Benedict and dill and artichoke omelette. Lunch, served until 3 P.M., is also available, but breakfast remains the main attraction. The restaurant occupies an old home at 1785 W. Lake Boulevard, 2 miles south of the center of town. To avoid the long weekend wait, time your arrival for the 7 A.M. opening. Call (530) 583-0871 for more information.

Aspens in Page Meadows

Important Phone Numbers & Websites

PHONE NUMBERS

Avalanche Conditions . . . . (530) 587-2158

Emergency 911

Highway Patrol—California
Truckee . . . . (530) 582-7570
South Lake Tahoe . . . . (530) 577-1001

Highway Patrol—Nevada . . . . (775) 688-2500

Road Conditions—California
In California . . . . (800) 427-7623 ((800) 427-ROAD)
From Outside California . . . . . . (916) 445-7623

Road Conditions—Nevada . . . . . . (877) 687-6237 ((877) NVROADS)

Sheriff—California
Alpine County . . . . (530) 694-2231
El Dorado County . . . . (530) 621-5655
Nevada County . . . . (530) 582-7838
Placer County . . . . (530) 889-7800

Sheriff—Nevada
Carson City . . . . (775) 887-2500
Douglas County . . . . (775) 782-9900
Washoe County . . . . (775) 328-3001

Sno-Park Program . . . . (916) 324-1222

WEB SITES

Caltrans Road Report: www.dot.ca.gov/hq/roadinfo

Central Sierra Snow Condition Report:
www.fs.fed.us/r5/tahoe/documents/avalanche/current_advisory.htm

Eldorado National Forest: www.fs.fed.us/r5/eldorado

Humboldt-Toiyabe National Forest: www.fs.fed.us/r4/htnf

Lake Tahoe Basin Management Unit: www.fs.fed.us/r5/ltbmu

National Weather Service: www.nws.noaa.gov

NDOT Road Report: www.nevadadot.com/traveler/roads

Tahoe National Forest: www.fs.fed.us/r5/tahoe

Weather Channel: www.weather.com

Wilderness Press: www.wildernesspress.com

APPENDIX II

Forest Service Listings

ELDORADO NATIONAL FOREST

Supervisor's Office
100 Forest Road
Placerville, CA 95667
(530) 622-5061

Amador Ranger District
26820 Silver Drive & Hwy 88
Star Route 3
Pioneer, CA 95666
(209) 295-4251

Placerville Ranger District
4060 Eight Mile Road
Camino, CA 95709
(530) 644-2324

Georgetown Ranger District
7600 Wentworth Springs Road
Georgetown, CA 95634
(530) 333-4312

Pacific Ranger District
7887 Highway 50
Pollock Pines, CA 95726
(530) 644-2349

LAKE TAHOE BASIN MANAGEMENT UNIT

Lake Tahoe Basin
Management Unit
35 College Drive
South Lake Tahoe, CA 96150
(530) 543-2600

TAHOE NATIONAL FOREST

TNF Headquarters
631 Coyote Street
Nevada City, CA 95959
(530) 265-4531

Downieville Ranger District
North Yuba Ranger Station
15924 Highway 49
Camptonville, CA 95922
(530) 288-3231

Foresthill Ranger District
22830 Foresthill Road
Foresthill, CA 95361
(530) 367-2224

Truckee Ranger District
9646 Donner Pass Road
Truckee, CA 96161
(530) 587-3558

TOIYABE NATIONAL FOREST

Supervisor's Office
1200 Franklin Way
Sparks, NV 89431
(775) 331-6444

Carson Ranger District
1536 S. Carson Street
Carson City, NV 89701
(775) 882-2766

APPENDIX III

Snowshoe Manufacturers

Atlas Snowshoe Co.
115 Tenth Street
San Francisco, CA 94103
(888) 48-ATLAS
fax: (415) 252-0354
email: questions@atlassnowshoe.com
www.atlassnowshoe.com

C3-Design Innovation
Verts
6146 So. 350 West
Salt Lake City, UT 84107
(801) 281-1331
fax: (801) 281-1333
email: sales@verts.com
www.verts.com

Crescent Moon
1199 Crestmoor
Boulder, CO 80303
(800) 587-7655
fax: (303) 499-2645
email: jakeroll@crescentmoonsnowshoes.com
www.crescentmoonsnowshoes.com

MSR—Mountain Safety Research
4000 First Avenue
Seattle, WA 98134
(800) 531-9531
fax: (800) 583-7583
email: info@msrgear.com
www.msrcorp.com

Northern Lites
300 S. 86th Avenue
Wausau, WI 54401
(800) 360-LITE
fax: (715) 848-0386
email: snowshoe@northernlites.com
www.northernlites.com

Redfeather
4705-A Oakland Street
Denver, CO 80239
(800) 525-0081
fax: (303) 375-0357
email: rfsnowshoes@earthlink.net
www.redfeather.com

Sherpa Snowshoes
9460 So. 60th Street
Franklin, WI 53132
(800) 621-2277 (Christy)
fax: (414) 423-9806
email: kmarkiewicz@idealmfgsolutions.com
www.sherpasnowshoes.com

Tubbs Snowshoe Co.
52 River Road
Stowe, VT 05672
(800) 882-2748 or (802) 253-7398
fax: (802) 253-9982
email: info@tubbssnowshoes.com
www.tubbssnowshoes.com

APPENDIX IV

Suggested Reading

Browning, Peter. 1991. *Place Names of the Sierra Nevada*. Berkeley: Wilderness Press.

Castle, Ken. 1997. *Tahoe*. San Francisco: Foghorn Press.

Darvill, M.D., Fred. 1998. *Mountaineering Medicine*. Berkeley: Wilderness Press.

Farquhar, Francis 1965. *History of the Sierra Nevada*. Berkeley: University of California Press.

Fredston, Jill & Doug Fesler. 1999. *Snow Sense: A Guide to Evaluating Snow Avalanche Hazard*. 4th Edition. Alaska Mountain Safety Center, Inc.

Graydon, Don & Curt Hanson, editors. 1997. *Mountaineering: The Freedom of the Hills*. 6th Edition. Seattle: The Mountaineers.

Hauserman, Tim. 2002. *The Tahoe Rim Trail*. Berkeley: Wilderness Press.

LaChapelle, Ed. 1985. *ABC of Avalanche Safety*. 2nd Edition. Seattle: The Mountaineers.

Lekisch, Barbara. 1988. *Tahoe Place Names*. Lafayette, CA: Great West Books.

Libkind, Marcus. 1995. *Ski Tours in the Sierra Nevada, Volume 1, Lake Tahoe*. 2nd Edition. Livermore, CA: Bittersweet Publishing Company.

O'Bannon, Allen & Mike Clelland. 1996. *Allen & Mike's Really Cool Backcountry Ski Book*. Evergreen, CO: Chockstone Press.

Prater, Gene. Edited by Dave Felkey. 1997. *Snowshoeing*. 4th Edition. Seattle: The Mountaineers.

Schaffer, Jeffrey P. 1998. *The Tahoe Sierra*. 4th Edition. Berkeley: Wilderness Press.

White, Michael C. 1999. *Snowshoe Trails of Yosemite*. Berkeley: Wilderness Press.

White, Mike. 2004. *Backpacking Nevada*. Berkeley: Wilderness Press.

White, Mike. 2005. *Best Snowshoe Trails of California*. 2nd Edition. Berkeley: Wilderness Press.

White, Mike. 2004. *Top Trails Lake Tahoe*. Berkeley: Wilderness Press.

Wilkerson, M.D., James A. 1983. *Medicine for Mountaineering*. 2nd Edition. Seattle: The Mountaineers.

Index

About the Author

Mike White was born and raised in Portland, Oregon. He learned to hike and snowshoe in the Cascades, and honed these outdoor skills while attending Seattle Pacific University. After college, Mike relocated to the high desert of Nevada, where he was drawn to the beauty of the Sierra in both summer and winter.

In the early 1990s, Mike began writing about the outdoors full time. He expanded Wilderness Press's *The Trinity Alps*. He then authored *Nevada Wilderness Areas and Great Basin National Park*, followed by the *Snowshoe Trails* series, *Sequoia National Park*, *Kings Canyon National Park*, *Backpacking Nevada*, *Top Trails Lake Tahoe*, and *Afoot & Afield Reno/Lake Tahoe*. Mike also contributed to *Backpacking California*, and has written for *Sunset* and *Backpacker* magazines and the *Reno Gazette-Journal*. He teaches backpacking and snowshoeing at Truckee Meadows Community College. Mike lives in Reno with his wife, Robin, and their two boys, David and Stephen, along with their yellow lab, Barkley.

Other Snowshoeing Titles
Available from Wilderness Press

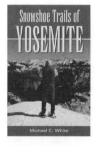

Snowshoe Trails of Yosemite

The easiest way to see El Capitan, Half Dome, and Glacier Point in all their winter glory is on these 41 trips in greater Yosemite, selected for their great scenery and ease of accessibility. Includes maps, directions, difficulty ratings, and "warm up" suggestions.

ISBN: 0-89997-253-5

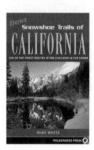

Best Snowshoe Trails of California

Experience the finest winter trekking in California's Sierra and Cascade mountain ranges. Covers 100 trips in Mt. Shasta, Lassen Volcanic National Park, Lake Tahoe, Yosemite, and Kings Canyon and Sequoia national parks. Includes maps, directions, difficulty ratings, and "warm up" suggestions.

ISBN 0-89997-364-7

For ordering information, call your local bookseller
or visit Wilderness Press at www.wildernesspress.com.